TROUBADOUR AND POET:
The Magical Ministry of Ric Masten

BY STEPHEN D. EDINGTON
With RIC MASTEN

Foreword By RUBY DEE

Order this book online at www.trafford.com/07-0876
or email orders@trafford.com

Most Trafford titles are also available at major online book retailers.

© Copyright 2007 Stephen D. Edington.
All rights reserved. No part of this publication may be reproduced, stored in a retrieval system, or transmitted, in any form or by any means, electronic, mechanical, photocopying, recording, or otherwise, without the written prior permission of the author.

Cover Design/Artwork by Richard Widhu
Photography by Cara Weston

Permissions
All poems by Ric Masten used by permission of Ric Masten.
"Waiting" and "Celebration" used by permission of Billie Barbara Masten.
"To My Dad" used by permission of Ellen Masten.
"Daddy, Walk With Me" used by permission of Jerraldine Masten.
"GH" and "The Other Universe" used by permission of Stuart Masten.

Note for Librarians: A cataloguing record for this book is available from Library and Archives Canada at www.collectionscanada.ca/amicus/index-e.html

Printed in Victoria, BC, Canada.

ISBN: 978-1-4251-2608-7

We at Trafford believe that it is the responsibility of us all, as both individuals and corporations, to make choices that are environmentally and socially sound. You, in turn, are supporting this responsible conduct each time you purchase a Trafford book, or make use of our publishing services. To find out how you are helping, please visit www.trafford.com/responsiblepublishing.html

Our mission is to efficiently provide the world's finest, most comprehensive book publishing service, enabling every author to experience success. To find out how to publish your book, your way, and have it available worldwide, visit us online at www.trafford.com/10510

 www.trafford.com

North America & international
toll-free: 1 888 232 4444 (USA & Canada)
phone: 250 383 6864 ♦ fax: 250 383 6804 ♦ email: info@trafford.com

The United Kingdom & Europe
phone: +44 (0)1865 722 113 ♦ local rate: 0845 230 9601
facsimile: +44 (0)1865 722 868 ♦ email: info.uk@trafford.com

10 9 8 7 6 5 4 3

*This book is dedicated to all of those
who have been touched and blessed
by the
Ministry of Ric Masten*

Acknowledgements

Since I've only known Ric Masten since the year 2000 I've had to rely on the memories, stories, and collected materials of many others in attempting to tell the story of his troubadour ministry with the Unitarian Universalists, as well as the ways in which his story has gone well beyond the UU community. For this reason I am indebted to a great number of individuals who have helped me bring his story to life. With the clear risk of overlooking some of them I offer the following heartfelt thanks:

First of all I thank Ric Masten for the many hours he spent with me at his home just south of Carmel, California in Palo Colorado Canyon. I've enjoyed every bit of the time we spent there. Thanks as well to Billie Barbara Masten for her stories and her hospitality. Ric and Billie's daughters Jerraldine, Ellen, and April have graciously contributed to this work, and April was especially helpful in editing the *Family Matters* chapter. Stuart Masten contributed two of his poems, for which I thank him.

Four of my colleagues in the Unitarian Universalist ministry, Revs. Glenn Turner, Rolfe Gerhardt, John Buehrens, and Elizabeth Miller agreed to be interviewed for this book, and were very generous with their time. I thank them all. Glenn and Rolfe also granted me use of the materials they've kept on Ric over the years. Rev. Ron Cook, another UU minister and Ric's neighbor in Palo Colorado Canyon, provided me with some very good information about Ric's entry into the UU ministry, and helped with the fact checking in Chapter Two.

Another great source of information for me has been Rosemary Matson, Ric and Billie's friend and nearby neighbor in Carmel Valley. It was Rosemary and her late husband, Rev. Howard Matson, who were instrumental in getting Ric's career as a UU troubadour minister launched. Rosemary offered a very thorough interview, as well as a treasure trove of material she's collected on Ric over the past 40 years.

I was also very reliant on many of Ric's ministerial colleagues, each of whom had their stories and tributes to offer. I thank all of them who responded to my inquiries by e-mails, letters, or phone calls: Revs. Mwalimu Imara, Carl Scovel, Robert Swain, John Frykman, Tom Owen-Towle, Robert Eddy, and Ken Brown.

Thanks also to Orloff Miller, Jr., Lars Frykman, and Paulette Lynch for offering their stories of Ric.

My sister and brother-in-law, Revs. Rose Edington and Melvin Hoover, helped me correct and edit the text; as did Frank Messar. My thanks to each of them.

Richard Widhu designed the beautiful cover for this book. The cover photograph of Ric is by Cara Weston, whom I thank for its use. Thanks to Michele Edington for the photo on the back cover.

My wife, Michele, has had to endure the self-absorbed ways I get into when I'm in book-writing mode. I am grateful for her forbearance and support. I have also relied on her computer skills, which more than offset my techo-illiteracy, in maintaining some semblance of order and process as I wrote this. Thanks, Hon.

Table of Contents

FOREWORD BY RUBY DEE......................ix

PREFACE
    A CRACK IN THE CONSCIOUSNESS....................xi

CHAPTER ONE:
    THE RAINBOW ZEN TRUCK STOP 1

CHAPTER TWO:
    WHO WAS THAT GUY? 11

CHAPTER THREE:
    THE MINISTER/POET—HOW EXPOSED
    AND VULNERABLE? 23

CHAPTER FOUR:
    THE MINISTER/POET—AS PASTOR 37

CHAPTER FIVE:
    THE MINISTER/POET—AS PROPHET 53

CHAPTER SIX:
    THE MINISTER/POET—AS THEOLOGIAN..............71

CHAPTER SEVEN:
    THE MINISTER/POET—AS COLLEAGUE 85

CHAPTER EIGHT:
    THE MINISTER/POET—FAMILY MATTERS 101

CHAPTER NINE:
    "THE MINISTRY FOR WHICH I'VE BEEN
    PREPARING ALL MY LIFE" 125

CHAPTER 10:
    THE MINISTRY BEYOND THE MINISTRY 143

CHAPTER ELEVEN:
    A TASTE OF CILANTRO. 161

FOREWORD

By
Ruby Dee

Over and over, Ossie and I had promised ourselves to get together with Ric and Billie Barbara, especially when the two of us expected to be on the West Coast with a couple of extra days meant just for visiting them in Big Sur. We imagined we'd have non-stop word work to do—I don't know—between the anticipations, the over talking and laughing. There would be silences, too, except for Ric and his daughter on guitars.

We'd met Ric a blurred age ago. One day our daughter, Hasna, came running into where we were reading a magazine and suddenly she said, "Hey Ma, Dad, listen, listen to this." Then she rocked with the kind of laughter that hunted us across the room and read one of Ric's poems. From that moment on, I was hooked on his contagious joy and righteous audacity.

Those words—impish, holy, wise, devilish, rebellious—snatched me to the edge of his aura for a fleeting peek inside. And in that peek I sensed a kindred spirit, a fellow lover of words—of the rhythms, the juxtapositions, the sounds of the vowels and consonants, uttered best out loud, and often, as warnings of the constant contradictions that could confuse our species. He is a master of the slyly ridiculous, the "see-ree-us", too—philosopher, humorist, overriding tears, fears, fight and moving out with belief in the glorious possibilities.

I count among my treasured books a copy of *Speaking Poems* signed by Ric when we first met in Harlem almost 30 years ago. It, like those I have collected since, is dog-eared and starred with favorites—some of which you'll find woven into the story of Ric's life which you hold in your hands now.

You'll be as delighted as I am that Stephen Edington has captured, in these pages, the spirit that has enabled Ric to triumph time and time again, and to coax us out of our comfort zones and into the mirror for a good look at ourselves. It is this spirit that enables Ric, even now, to live life to the last drop.

I can't imagine the end of Ric Masten. We who know and love him, and countless new ones of us waiting in the wings, will forever ride the wave of words he has given us to sing and to say out loud—even to ourselves. How wonderful to have this book as companion and context.

Ossie and I never made it to Big Sur, but I still imagine guitars, the four of us sitting under the majestic sky, talking, laughing, singing, shouting out new mind equations. I know Ossie would be as impressed as I am with this telling of Ric's story, this magic lens on life and love and poetry in Divine motion.

Enjoy!

Ruby Dee
May 2007

PREFACE

A Crack in the Consciousness

The day after Jack Kerouac died the poet Allen Ginsberg was asked at a gathering of students at Yale University, for whom he was doing a poetry reading, what he felt was the real significance of Kerouac's life. Twelve years after the publication of *On the Road* the author of this "Beat Bible" had died in alcoholic obscurity, feeling estranged and largely alienated from many of the cultural upheavals his signature novel had triggered. The question behind the student's question was, essentially, "So what was so great about Kerouac anyway?"

After several seconds of meditative silence Ginsberg replied, "He provided a crack in the consciousness." The consciousness to which Ginsberg was referring was the overarching cultural mindset of post-World War II America in the 1950s. It was through the crack Kerouac pried open, Allen noted, that whole new levels of awareness—artistic, poetic, musical, literary, and political—flowed into American society and culture in ways that Kerouac himself had scarcely envisioned. The times were ready for the message and mood he'd delivered. He left it to others to continue the song.

Ric Masten is hardly facing alcoholic destruction and demise, a la Jack Kerouac. But I feel an assessment of the unique kind of ministry he has provided within the liberal religious movement of Unitarian Universalism can be aptly summarized in the same terms Ginsberg used in assessing Kerouac. Ric Masten provided a crack in the consciousness of a religious organization.

In Ric's case the crack in the consciousness he brought about pried open any number of assumptions about the meaning and style of the Unitarian Universalist ministry in the late 1960s and early 70s. This rather scruffy looking red-bearded guy, who was without even a college education, much less a seminary degree, and who was pushing 40 at the time, began showing up in UU congregations and at UU sponsored college events singing his songs and speaking his poems as the sixties were winding down. In time enough Unitarian Universalists came to regard him as a minister, and the Unitarian Universalist Association conferred that standing upon him. Within the culture of the Unitarian Universalist ministry of that time, Ric became the counter-cultural minister. One of the roles of a counter-cultural force, presence, or personality is to both challenge and transform the mainstream culture it stands alongside. It is, in Ginsberg's words again, to provide a crack in the consciousness of the predominant culture in order that change and transformation can take place.

Ric Masten would be the last person to claim sole credit for the many and varied currents of change that have swept across the Unitarian Universalist landscape over the past three to four decades since he was accepted into its ministry. I make no such claim on his behalf either. At the same time the role he has played in the re-shaping and re-visioning of the UU ministry, as carried forth by the professional clergy and laypeople alike, cannot be ignored. His way with words, and his overall presence before a UU (or other) gathering in a church, or at a school, or on a college campus or jail or mental health facility, had a rather magical way of bringing together the mind, spirit, and soul of his listeners. The Masten presence alone offered a challenge to the heavily intellectual and largely "head-based" style of Unitarian Universalism that was predominant in the movement following the creation of the Unitarian Universalist Association in 1961. In seeking to bring together the mind, heart, and spirit in his appearances Ric was offering a more wholistic kind of ministry than was found in many of our congregations at the time.

I first met Ric very briefly at the Unitarian Church of All Souls in New York City in the spring of 1991. I was helping chaperone a high school youth group trip from my church in Nashua, New Hampshire, and we were bunking in at All Souls. As we were heading out one evening, Rev. John Buehrens, who was Co-Minister there with Rev. Forrest Church at the time, caught me in the hallway and asked if I'd like to meet Ric Masten. Our introduction was a very quick "How are ya, good to meet ya, like your stuff," kind of encounter. Ric had a roomful of people waiting for him to go on and I had a bunch of kids who wanted to go out on the town. Had I known Ric was going to be in town I'd have made his gig part of our itinerary. By the time I got back later that evening the show was over and Ric was long gone.

Some eight or nine years went by before we re-connected. This time I was in Monterey, California visiting a good friend and fellow Beat Generation aficionado and enthusiast named Jerry Cimino. He was running a little shop in Monterey at the time called The Beat Museum, which he has since moved to San Francisco. Jerry asked me if I'd like to take a run down to Big Sur with him the next day so he could pick up some books from a local poet whose works he stocked. "He doesn't really consider himself a Beat," as Jerry explained it to me, "But a lot of his stuff has a kind of Beat flavor to it. You probably wouldn't mistake him for Allen Ginsberg, but he is good. In fact, he was recently named the Poet Laureate of Carmel, California."

It sounded fine to me. How many chances, after all, does one get to meet the Poet Laureate of Carmel? "He's on chemotherapy right now so I'll have to call ahead to see when would be a good time for us to stop by," Jerry continued. And then he added, "Since you live on the East Coast you've probably never heard of him. His name is Ric Masten."

Whoa. Ric Masten? As in the Unitarian Universalist minister, troubadour, poet, songster guy, who wrote *Let It Be A Dance? That* Ric Masten? Jerry didn't even know about the UU minister part but all my other descriptions clicked with him and we very quickly realized we each knew him, albeit in different contexts. The next day, with Jerry at the wheel, I made what would prove to be the first of many trips up Palo Colorado Canyon to the home of Ric and Billie Barbara Masten.

As Jerry had noted, Ric was at the height of his chemotherapy treatments at the time for prostate cancer. He also had hip replacement surgery pending. Since his house was built on the side of the hill, and with its rooms positioned on several different levels, Ric had aluminum walkers placed in many of the doorways to make getting around a bit easier for him. When I was able to make a return visit there about a year and a half later, while attending a conference near by, the change was remarkable. The chemo regimen was over. The hip had been replaced, and Ric was getting around with just the help of a wooden carved-stick cane. The cancer had not been vanquished—nor will it ever be—but it had at least been tamped down a little.

It had been tamped down, in fact, to the point that soon after our second visit Ric was ready to hit the road again. He's stopped carrying his guitar, but his poems are still there and still as good as ever. And now he has a whole new genre of "cancer poems" written in that same slightly off-beat, slightly irreverent, but still cutting-to-the-core fashion, that has characterized his work over the years.

On his second East Coast tour, after his taking to the road again, I was fortunate enough to have Ric in my church in Nashua, New Hampshire for both a Sunday service and an afternoon reading. We drew people who had been reading, singing, and loving his poems and songs for years, and others for whom the name Ric Masten had meant nothing until seeing it on a flyer. For all who showed up for both appearances the Masten magic was clearly still there.

Just before his Nashua visit the *UU World* magazine did a feature article on Ric which was written by Frances Gerra Whittelsey. It told of the unique kind of ministry he's had with UUs and others over the years, and about his much more recent outreach to various cancer survivor groups and organizations. As we discussed the article—with which Ric was very pleased—the idea of our collaborating on a book began to emerge. I rolled the idea around over the next several weeks and months. Then, with my wife along this time, we made the trip across the country to Palo Colorado Canyon to record as many of Ric's memories as we could get on tape in the course of a few days.

Ric Masten's ministry makes for a great story, as told not only by him but by many of the other clergy and laypeople who have played a role in it. But he and I want to do more than tell a story here—good as it is. Our hope is to use Ric's alternative, counter-cultural style of ministry to bring into better focus some insights his story offers for clergy and laity alike about the many meanings and the many challenges of ministry in the liberal religious tradition. If we can do that we will widen even further that crack in the consciousness.

Even with his current dealings with cancer Ric Masten would agree that he has fared much better than Kerouac did. Far from fading into a bitter kind of obscurity he has been able to both witness and be a part of the currents that flowed through the crack he helped pry open back in the late 1960s. To use his favorite metaphor, he has been able to both watch and take part in the dance he began for Unitarian Universalists so many years ago.

It is not possible to tell the story of another person's life while standing completely apart from your own. I inevitably see Ric's story through my own minister's eyes. If I were, say, a poet, or an artist, or a therapist, etc. I know I'd tell his story differently than I'll be doing here. Being a minister does not entirely define my life, and who I am, but it does provide the primary window through which I see Ric's life and work.

I also write out of a relationship that Ric and I have cultivated over just the past several years. I did not know him "back in the day" when his poetic, troubadour style of ministry had a much higher profile within the Unitarian Universalist community than it does now. My entry into the UU ministry did not happen until 1979. Being so situated, I hope, gives me enough closeness to Ric to appreciate him for the remarkable human being, and minister, that he is, while still leaving me enough distance from his 40 year career in the UU movement to offer a fair assessment of it.

Both poets and ministers search for words that they hope will touch the minds and hearts of their readers and hearers. This is the same hope that Ric and I share for the readers of this book.

Stephen Edington
Nashua, New Hampshire

CHAPTER ONE:

The Rainbow Zen Truck Stop

it was just a rundown truck stop
a greasy spoon café
twenty years behind me now
seems like yesterday
I was on my way to somewhere
to pull off some big deal
like every kid of twenty
"the inventor of the wheel"
I had scrambled eggs and coffee
a piece of buttered toast
and the drivers at the counter
were more talkative than most

and when the subject wasn't women
they talked about the road
and the miles that they had traveled
and the weight of the load
funny...ain't it funny
how it all comes 'round again
it was just a roadside truck stop
and they called it Rainbow's End

and I sat there feelin' empty
as those poor devils spoke

if that was all there was to life
then it's a short length of rope
but remember I was twenty
and I've covered ground since then
I've picked up on philosophy
a Greek became my friend
I've looked into religion
read Sartrees and Camoose
been up on the mountain
with an old guru

and when the subject isn't women
they talk about the road
and the miles that they have traveled
and the weight of the load
funny...ain't it funny
how it all comes 'round again
it was just a roadside truck stop
and they called it Rainbow
Zen.

Rainbow Zen by Ric Masten

To arrive at Ric and Billie Barbara Masten's home is to feel like you've come about as close to the end of the rainbow as you'll ever get, or want to. The last mile, if you're driving it, is not a ride for the faint hearted. Once you make the left off the paved road by a long row of mailboxes you're navigating a very narrow strip of dirt, gravel, and ruts, with no guard-rail. The best way to manage it is to inhale at the mailboxes and exhale when you pull into the Masten driveway.

But the view is worth the drive. The vista from Ric's weather-worn deck as you look across the Big Sur mountains, on out to a little blue spot of the Pacific Ocean, has a certain Zen-like aura to it. In a single moment you feel like you've seen all you need to see to make your life complete. It is the way the world, at its best, is supposed to look. This has been Ric Masten's home from the time he was just a bit of ways beyond the "kid of twenty" he writes about in the above poem. And whether or not he's ready to acknowledge it, Ric has now become that "old guru...up on the mountain" himself.

The vista from Chez Masten is a little like the view Ric now has of the unfolding of our liberal religious movement—which goes by the name of Unitarian Universalism—since just after the time of the merger of those two denominations in 1961. It is the mountain top view of a liberal religious movement as it has played out over the past four decades.

By his own estimate Ric has come off this mountain enough times to appear in over 500 UU congregations, as well as at several General Assemblies, and various other UU gatherings and conferences far too numerous to name or recall. He has also cultivated relationships with scores of UU clergy during that time as his life has intersected with theirs in some very meaningful and humorous and often poignant ways.

He's done all this with his guitar over his shoulder or with a sheaf of his poems in hand and a store of stories in his head; and almost always with his playful and sometimes rascal-like self. But like any good playful rascal, Ric does not come down from his mountain just to play and be rascal-like. He comes to challenge, to provoke, to amuse, to startle, to soothe, and even at times to generate a little anger.

Ric Masten has been the one and only Unitarian Universalist troubadour minister. For all of his travels his many roads have always, in time, wound back to the home on the mountainside a ways out in Palo Colorado Canyon on the northern edge of California's Big Sur country. It is now time to take some measure; not just the measure of Ric's life but the measure of the life of the small but persistent liberal religious movement that he and I and so many of our colleagues and lay people have dedicated much of our lives to. What has it meant to be a part of the liberal ministry, on the part of clergy and laity alike, over the latter part of the past century, and into the new century and millennium now getting underway?

The usual way to make such an assessment is to create a Commission that would send out surveys and hold meetings and eventually issue a report that may or may not get widely read. Or we could see what the life and times of our resident poet, troubadour, and court jester might have to tell us. The alternative style of ministry Ric has offered us UUs for much of his life provides a unique lens through which to view where we've been, how we've done, and where we are now.

Why add the term "court jester" to that of poet and troubadour in describing Ric? Poet and troubadour are Ric's job description. It's what he does. Court jester speaks, in a broader sense, to the role he's played and continues to play for us. The role of the court jester, as is fairly well known, was not just to make the monarch—and, by extension, the established order he or she represented—laugh or be amused. A truly accomplished court jester was the one who would use wit and creativity to get just far enough under the skin of the monarch or establishment to provoke them or to give them an angle on an issue that they hadn't seen previously. A good court jester is one who delivers the "Ah-ha Moment" to the established order; which is also what a good poet or balladeer does.

Ric Masten, by way of his poems and his performances, has given many of those within the wider UU communion, and those who are also well beyond that communion, any number of "Ah-ha moments" over the course of his ministry. In the pages that follow some of those moments will be recalled—both the ones Ric has given as well as some of those he has received. But, as already noted, the intention here is not just to write a memoir, or a retrospective of Ric's life as seen both through his eyes and the eyes of others, interesting and valuable as that alone would be. What follows will, to be sure, contain elements of a memoir or retrospective. But our hope, both Ric's and mine, is that this book will also offer those of us who take both seriously and joyously the liberal religious journey a way of looking at ourselves and at what that journey of the spirit involves and means.

This is also a book about mortality, and of the need to preserve stories in the face of the mortality we all, in time, have to deal with. I was made aware of this need in the fall of 2005 while promoting the appearance Ric made at the church where I serve as minister. As I put out the word of his appearance to all the UU churches that are within a ninety minute drive from mine (and in my part of New England, that's a lot) I came to notice a certain demarcation. For those ministers and laypeople who were, say, above the age of 50, and who'd had a long-time association with our liberal religious movement, the response was along the lines of: "Ric Masten! Great! I'll make every effort to be there!" But with those—ministers and lay folk alike—in their mid-40s and younger, or who've not been in the UU fold all that long, the response was more vague. They knew Ric Masten was the guy who'd written "Let It Be A Dance"—number 311 in the *Singing the Living Tradition* hymnal—but knew very little of his story and of the role he has played in within Unitarian Universalism over the years. Beyond his signature hymn they also knew very little of his poetry.

Of course, each generation has its own story to tell, and each generation may or may not pay a whole lot of attention to the stories that have preceded it. But Ric Masten's story—both the way he remembers and tells it, and the way others who were a part of it remember and tell it—is something too valuable to be allowed to fade away unrecorded. One cannot have a future without having a past, and knowing what that past contains. The same goes for institutions and movements; they also have to know where they've been in order to have any clear sense of where they are going. Ric Masten's life and ministry offer a lens for seeing where we've been—which just might, we can hope, give us a sense of where we yet may go as a liberal religious movement in these early years of this 21st century.

Ric's life and ministry also offer a lens through which one can view some of the demands, challenges, and many paradoxes of the ministerial life. These are insights that ministers and lay folk alike, each from their own standpoint, can well appreciate and be enlightened by.

Ric became the Reverend Ric Masten under some very unique, and at the time controversial, circumstances. This is a story that will be told in more detail later, other than to say here that it came at a time when our UU Association was still very reluctant to acknowledge that there could be other forms of ministry in which one could meaningfully engage, besides that of the formal parish ministry for which one had to be formally and properly trained and educated. And yet, even as Ric has carried out his alternative style of ministry (which we would probably categorize as "Community Ministry" today) he's found himself having to deal with some of the same kinds of issues—albeit in a different context—that those of us operating in the more conventional styles of ministry also have to deal with. Let's consider just a few of them.

How much of my inner self and my inner struggles do I disclose to my congregation and how much do I hold back or take elsewhere? In the very first year of his ministry Ric wrote a poem about how close he came to suicide via a leap off Big Sur's Bixby Canyon Bridge. Ric read this poem at various UU gatherings at which he subsequently appeared after this trip to the Bixby Bridge. This nearly got him dismissed from the UU ministry before he was even three years into it by placing his approval for Final Fellowship in jeopardy. Here, too, is another story for another chapter; this one about how a minister stays on the side of the line that allows self-disclosure to be a means by which those who are a witness to it can find greater strength and renewed hope in their own lives.

Another important dimension to this self-disclosure issue for ministers is how much, and to what extent, should his/her family life be shared. How much attention and care Ric gave his children in their growing-up years, in the face of the demands—as well as his own ambitions—about his poet/troubadour/minister career is a piece of his life that also comes through in his poems. And when he and Billie Barbara each discovered, at one point in their lives, that they were pursuing extramarital affairs, it ended up becoming the subject of a shared work titled *His and Hers*. When it comes to both family and spousal life, Ric was positioned in a way that did allow him to offer a greater level of self-disclosure than his colleagues in the parish generally could. But he still had to face the issue that all clergy face, namely how much of my private life do I allow to also become my public life.

The heart of this issue is best illustrated—both in drawing and word—in a collection of Ric's poems titled *Stark Naked*. That's the question, isn't it? How stark naked can any of us risk being as we go about being ministers. And how naked, or covered, do those with whom we minister wish or need us to be.

Another matter, related to the above, is about ministry and the ego—more specifically, the ego of the minister. I will openly admit, as will most of my colleagues in their more honest moments, that to be a minister is to be a self-promoter. If we didn't feel we had something worth putting out there on Sunday mornings in our pulpits, then we wouldn't be doing it. We write and deliver our sermons because we want to be heard and listened to and taken seriously. Whatever the topic may be, every sermon we write and preach is about us in the sense that it represents something we have created and that we believe merits the time taken by those who hear it. In one way or another we are all repeating the title of one of Ric's collection of poems, *Notice Me*.

For the quite practical reason of having to make a living, self-promotion is something Ric has had to be more deliberate and up front about than his colleagues in more traditional forms of ministry. He's had to create his congregation from those who are drawn to his poems and songs and presentations. He's had to create his own publishing house to get his works out there. He has to schedule his own tours by playing on the contacts he's cultivated over the years. No agent is doing any of this for him. Ric would not have had the life and career he's had if he had not been a good and persistent self-promoter. Notice Me. Exactly.

This is the challenge of the "Notice Me Factor" for those in ministry as well as those who are ministered to and with. A good and able minister is one who believes deeply in him/herself. A minister must have a strong and vibrant ego. Most important, however, a good minister is one who has learned to live within the Zen-like paradox that ministry is all about me and nothing about me all at the same time. Ric's poems and music are all about him and the way he offers them. At the same time they would be nothing at all had they not also touched, blessed and challenged so many other lives over so many years.

So it is with ministry. Ministry is about the minister—in whatever form his or her ministry may take. But at the same time it has no meaning apart from the lives it has touched and blessed and challenged. There is no ministry apart from those who are ministered to. Ministry is hardly those things a minister does. It is instead a dance between the minister and the ministered to; and the lead in that dance is constantly changing. To examine the life and ministry of Ric Masten is to gain a clearer understanding about the dance of ministry.

Still another of the ongoing challenges and demands of the liberal ministry is speaking truth to power when it comes to the workings of the larger world in which one's ministry is taking place. It also means addressing those worldly workings in ways that bring greater illumination and understanding of them—even, or especially, to those of us who supposedly possess "enlightened" minds already. The heyday of Ric's troubadour ministry took place during the Civil Rights and Black Empowerment Movements, the Peace Movement of the Vietnam Era, and in the Women's Movement for both equality and liberation.

In addressing such matters as these, in poetry and song, Ric's truths were not only directed at the powers that be. They were just as often directed at those in the struggles themselves. Ric had a way of gently and even playfully pointing to some of the pitfalls and foibles and unexamined assumptions and unrealized self-righteousness of those who so earnestly strive to be on the right side of history.

Moving to a more personal level, those engaged in ministry will acknowledge that the times when they feel most inadequate and the most challenged occur when, as a minister, they are looked to for comfort, help and understanding in times of inexplicably cruel tragedies and losses. These are times when all you can offer is your presence; and then hope and pray that that is enough. And yet out of such moments come some of the greatest and most lasting rewards and returns of ministry itself. The circumstances around which Ric Masten came to write *Let It Be A Dance* were such a moment. A song that has lifted the hearts and spirits of hundreds, if not thousands, of people over the decades was originally written in response to a horrific automobile accident that claimed several young lives. It is one example of an ongoing phenomenon that any number of ministers can testify to, namely that some of life's greatest and most inexplicable tragedies can also provide the grounds for some of life's greatest blessings and transformations.

Finally, the ultimate demand of ministry, I would say, is to provide those with whom we minister, whatever the setting or context of one's ministry may be, a way of meaningfully dealing with their mortality. Indeed, one of our colleagues in the UU ministry, the Rev. Forrest Church, has defined religion—in what have now become oft cited words within the Unitarian Universalist movement—as "our human response to the dual reality of being alive and knowing that we shall die." Religion, understood in this manner, is the means by which we choose to be alive in the face of our finitude. I also believe this is the ultimate role of the artist, the poet, and the writer—to provide us ways of saying 'yes' to life in the face of the fleetingness of life. In February of 1999 Ric Masten was diagnosed with terminal prostate cancer. Granted, no living creature on earth has ever lived a "non-terminal" life; but our mortality does not usually become real until it is given a certain, and specific, focus.

Ric has been given that certain and specific focus. And with that focus he has taken his ministry of poetry and song and appearances into still another dimension over the past nine years. He partnered his poetic life with the insights of a clinical psychologist and fellow cancer survivor, Dr. Larry Lachman, to produce the book *Parallel Journeys*, subtitled "A Spirited Approach to Coping and Living with Cancer." Never one to confine his poetic/troubadour life and ministry to only the UU family, Ric has taken his ministry into the family of those living—and who are seeking and finding ways of meaningful living—with cancer. In his appearance before my congregation in October of 2005 I was struck by how he was able to address his dealings with prostate cancer in an open and honest way, but without it becoming the dominant motif of his message. The living-with-cancer part of Ric's life has become one more part of the larger mosaic of his life that has touched and blessed so many others.

> and when the subject isn't women
> they talk about the road
> and the miles that they have traveled
> and the weight of the load
> funny...ain't it funny
> how it all comes round again
> it was just a roadside truck stop
> and they called it Rainbow
> Zen.

Consider this book a stop-off at the Rainbow Zen Truck Stop. We'll talk of the road Ric Masten has traveled, and hear from some of those who have been a part of that trip. And we'll see what just might come round again.

CHAPTER TWO:

Who Was That Guy?

and now here I am before you...
now won't you take this chance
to jump upon the table
and join me in a dance.

From *Coffee Table Dancer* by Ric Masten

How did Ric Masten even get into the room at the Starr King School for the Ministry on that February day in 1971? He was asking the Unitarian Universalist Association's Ministerial Fellowship Committee to make him a credentialed UU minister. And yet he had no theological degree, no undergraduate college degree, no Clinical Pastoral Education, no internship experience—nothing at all, that is to say, that they were requiring of all the other candidates who came before them seeking entry into the UU ministry. In the words of his *Coffee Table Dancer* poem Ric was asking the MFC (and, by extension, the Unitarian Universalists) to take a chance on him, and to join *his* dance, since he certainly hadn't followed any of the dance steps they expected their candidates to step to.

Who *was* that guy? More to the point, who did he think he was showing up in such a place and under such conditions? Like the song says, it was a long and winding road that led Ric Masten to that little brick building of a seminary on Berkeley's LeConte Avenue.

There are any number of places where we can pick up that long and winding road. One place is the curve a lot of people find themselves coming into as they come into early adulthood. They look up the road and wonder if there is a religious and spiritual community for them, maybe up around the next bend someplace, where they might actually fit in. Many of the stories people in UU congregations tell about how they became Unitarian Universalists begin at that point on their road. Such was the case with Ric and Billie Barbara Bolton Masten in the mid-1960s. As Ric tells it:

"I was an aspiring folk singer at the time and had even sung with Joan Baez at one of the Big Sur Folk Festivals. I'd gotten into a big fight with a good friend of mine that disturbed me so much I got to thinking that maybe there was something wrong with me spiritually, or that I needed to do some kind of spiritual work, or something like that. So Billie and I decided to try to find ourselves a church. Billie had been raised Church of Christ fundamentalist and had long been disenchanted with her religion; and I'd been brought up with hardly any kind of formal religious education at all. We decided we'd try out every church on the Monterey Peninsula, taking them in alphabetical order from the yellow pages in the phone book. My poor kids had to go to a different Sunday School every Sunday for three years!

"Eventually we worked our way along to the Methodists. On that Sunday we were parked in Monterey with the Sunday paper, reading the listings for the Sunday services and trying to figure out where the Methodists were located. Then an ad for the Unitarian Universalist Church in Monterey caught my eye. The sermon title was *Are We Actors or Are We Authors?* and the minister was Rev. Bob O'Brien. I said to Billie, 'Let's skip the Methodists for this Sunday because I'd like to know the answer to this.' So we went to the Unitarian Universalist Church. Bob never quite answered the question in his sermon, but I got it that his point was to make us think on the question for ourselves rather than hand us The Answer. We became UUs that day, and Bob and I went on to become good friends."

By now Ric and Billie Barbara were living in their still evolving Palo Colorado Canyon home which Ric was building himself using his carpentry skills. He'd bought the land with the help of a small inheritance and decided he'd try to make it as a poet and singer. He'd quit his jobs and had gone off with his family to Big Sur to, in his words, "do a kind of hippie thing in the bushes with a bone around my neck."

This was not exactly the life Ric's parents, his mother in particular, had envisioned for him. His father, Richard T. Masten, who owned and edited a Carmel newspaper, died when Ric was 12. His mother, Hildreth, remarried an optometrist, Dr. Chester Hare. (More on Ric's family in Chapter 8). Ric was packed off to boarding school as an adolescent and then went on to flunk out of four colleges and drop out of a fifth. While his IQ tests put him at 106, Ric later learned that he unknowingly had severe dyslexia as well as a hearing impairment. But at the time all he could conclude was that he was stupid.

He did discover, however, an aptitude for art to which his mother responded by sending him, in 1947, to Paris for two years to study at the Institute des Beaux Arts. This, too, proved to be a dead end and he came home and put his brushes aside. Returning from Europe, Ric teamed up with a couple of friends who began writing and producing musical comedies for a local community theater, which is where he met and eventually married Billie Barbara Bolton. As the children came along he worked at construction jobs in Carmel and in a print shop in Monterey while trying to make a go of it as a song writer and singer. This led to his working for Warner Brothers for a time, and releasing such memorable tunes as *Rockabilly Blues*, *Teen Age Creature*, and *Baby, Baby, Baby You're a Thinking Man's Gal*. There are many roads to the UU ministry. Some of them are certainly stranger than others!

This road came to a clear fork, however, when Ric's attempts to balance his make-a-living jobs and his musical career left his family severely shortchanged when it came to getting much of his time. Warner Brothers wanted him to move to Los Angeles but Billie wanted more of him at home. This led to the decision to make the move to Palo Colorado Canyon, build a house, raise what food for themselves that they could, and for Ric to try to make it as a poet and song-writer—while also working for his father-in-law as a cement finisher as the need dictated. It was about this time, in 1967, that the confluence of Ric's poetry and songs, his homesteading in Palo Colorado Canyon, and his joining the Carmel Unitarian Universalist Church (real name: The Unitarian Universalist Church of the Monterey Peninsula) came together and pointed his road towards the Unitarian Universalist ministry.

Rosemary Matson is a near life-long UU, a member of the Carmel/Monterey UU Church, the widow of the Rev. Howard Matson, and the 1986 recipient of the Unitarian Universalist Association's Annual Holmes-Weatherly Award for social justice. She currently lives in Carmel Valley. Given her theology one would be hard put to convince Rosemary of the existence of angels—angels in any celestial sense anyway. But if an angel is one who appears at a crucial point in our life journey, and opens up a transforming path for us, then Ms. Matson, and her late husband Howard, played just that role in Ric Masten's life. This is Rosemary's account of how she helped place Ric on the path to ministry:

"Howard was an Associate Minister at the San Francisco UU Church and I was on the staff of the Starr King School, working in Development and Public Relations. I was also the Settlement Director for the Pacific Central District—the first woman to have that position. Howard and Bob O'Brien were very close when Bob was the minister in Carmel. We were house-sitting for a member of the Carmel congregation and got invited to a luau boar-roast at the Mastens, who had become part of a couples group at the church. We got there and the boar was in the ground smoking away surrounded by a lot of hungry people drinking beer. When Ric found out that Howard was a UU minister he said, 'Come on into the house. I want to show you some stuff.' So Howard and I went in and Ric got out his guitar and we sat on the floor of the living room while he started playing and singing. And Howard said, 'Man, these are sermons you're singing!' He was really taken with the content of the songs.

"In less than a half-hour there was a whole circle of people sitting on the floor behind Ric listening to his songs. I could see they were entranced. So that was the key. From that experience Howard and I started working on the churches in the District to get Ric to come and present a program to their congregations—either as a Sunday service or in some other setting."

But Rosemary and Howard weren't satisfied with just getting Ric in front of UU congregations in the Pacific Central District, and in following his doings on the local Carmel/Monterey folk and poetry scene. They saw in him someone who could reach that young adult, college age population which has long proven to be so elusive to Unitarian Universalists as well as to most major mainline Protestant denominations. How about getting Ric onto college campuses by way of near-by UU churches?

But Ric's poems didn't fit the mold, as it were, of what academically oriented, university English Department types considered "real poetry." And his informal, slightly irreverent, and somewhere-between-Beat-and-Hippie demeanor was hardly that of visiting college lecturer. All the more reason, therefore, to make Ric Masten a Unitarian Universalist Billings Lecturer!

At that time the UUA had a fund set up for what was called the Billings Lectureship. Its purpose was to place Unitarian Universalist speakers on college campuses to offer presentations that would promote UUism. These appearances could be arranged directly with the colleges or universities, but were more commonly set up through the local UU church, with the church's minister usually acting as the agent. They were also arranged through the Unitarian Universalist campus ministry organization of that day, the Student Religious Liberals.

If the intent of the Billings Lectureship was to present Unitarian Universalism as an academically respectable and intellectually defensible religion, Ric Masten was probably not quite what the founders of this fund had in mind. Ric was, and is, neither anti-intellectual nor anti-academic (his five failed attempts at being a college student notwithstanding); but he was clearly not a stand behind the podium and deliver a carefully prepared lecture kind of guy. He relied on his "speaking poems," which are meant more for the ear than the page, his guitar, and his innate charm to carry him along in front of an audience instead of a manuscript for a lecture. Could this troubadour poet and folk singer, who had only recently stumbled across UUism by way of a newspaper ad, be sold to the powers that be at the UUA as a guy to spend Billings money on?

Howard and Rosemary asked an old friend, Ron Cook, to meet and hear Ric do his thing at the Palo Alto UU Church. Ron worked in the UUA's Department of Adult Programs. He also administered the Billings Lectureship and was the Director of Student Religious Liberals. That night at the church, with the leaders of SRL present, they agreed that Ric was who they wanted as the Billings Lecturer. Ray Hopkins, the Executive Vice President of the UUA, approved the first of its kind program in which Billings money would pay a lecturer a year's salary and travel expenses.

The next step for Rosemary was to introduce Ric to the Unitarian Universalists of North America. She asked her old friend, Bob Hohler, Director of the Layman's League, to sponsor an evening with Ric for the entire General Assembly in Cleveland in 1968.

This was before the GA reached its present state where a great multiplicity of workshops, presentations, worship services, and lectures are simultaneously scheduled. In 1968 Ric had the whole gathering to himself for the time that he was on. He was such a hit at that General Assembly that a lot of UU ministers wanted Ric to represent the movement on their local college campuses and at their churches. All Ron had to do was create Ric's travel schedule for his first year on the Billings circuit.

Shortly after this Ron left the UUA staff to teach at the Starr King School for the Ministry, but by then Ric had made so many friends among the UU ministers that he was able to set up his "lectures" by himself and with their help. Among that early cadre of ministers who served as Ric's agents, so to speak, were Ralph Stutzman, Alan Deale, Chuck Eddis, Bob Swain. Rolfe Gerhardt, Fred LaShane, Dave Johnson, Ernie Pipes, Chris Raible, Gordon Gibson, Chuck Reinhardt, Glenn Turner, David Weissbard, Richard Gilbert, John Buehrens, Robert Fulghum, and doubtless many more too numerous to name here.

Looking back on it, Ron Cook sees a wry irony in that having the full financial backing of an establishment like the UUA gave Ric the means to affect an outside-the-establishment, counter-cultural type of wanderer. The credit, in this case however, really goes to the UUA—and to people like Ron Cook—for their willingness to think and act outside the box in bringing a liberal religious voice and presence to a segment of the population they may not have otherwise reached. After relocating to the West Coast, Ron also bought some land in Palo Colorado Canyon, and in time, and with Ric's help, built the house where he and his wife live today. As Ron puts it, "I helped get Ric going and he helped me build my house." The two remain good friends and neighbors.

Rosemary Matson also continued to use Ric's services and talents in ways that worked to both her and his advantage. In her capacity as Development Director for the Starr King School for the Ministry, Rosemary arranged for Ric to cut an album which would then be sold by the SKSM Auxiliary. As Ms. Matson tells it: "The President then, Bob Kimble, didn't quite know what I was doing. But I had a SKSM Auxiliary where I'd get Starr King students to go speak to UU women's groups. This way I hooked them, and when those little old ladies died they left SKSM in their will. So, one of my projects was to get the SKSM Auxiliary to sell Ric records for scholarships and Ric got a dollar a record for all we sold." Taking a cue from her husband's remark when he first heard Ric sing ("Man, these are sermons you're singing!") the first Masten album was called *Twelve String Sermons*. Among the songs on it were ones that would become Ric Masten classics including *Coffee Table Dancer*, *Notice Me*, and *Who's Wavin'* (*To Stevie—From the Shore*). According to Rosemary SKSM cut four or five more albums of Ric's, and as he became more well known around the Association the UUA stepped in and started making his records.

Indeed, Ric Masten's profile was on the ascendancy in the UUA during the late 1960s even though the Billings funds abruptly ran out after a couple of years. So abruptly, in fact, that Ric got the word while on tour in Tacoma, Washington that the UUA could no longer continue to support him other than to buy him a plane ticket back to Monterey! But through the efforts of Vice Moderator Margaret Hansen, and the UUA's Department of Education, with Norm Benson as Executive Director, the Association did pick up Ric's sponsorship for an additional length of time. This gave Ric the time, as just noted, to develop enough relationships and contacts with UU clergy that he was able to continue his troubadour poet career with the UUs on his own.

It was Ric Masten's travels on the Billings and post-Billings circuits, his appearances at a couple of General Assemblies (1968 and 1969), his albums and appearances on behalf of the Starr King School, and his cultivation of relationships with UU clergy and lay leaders across the Association, that led the Coffee Table Dancer to the table at which the members of the UUA's Ministerial Fellowship Committee, circa 1971, were seated at the Starr King School. In the course of his travels on behalf, and with the support, of the UUA Ric concluded that what he was doing was indeed a ministry.

Granted, the many and varied labors of love that thousands of UU laypeople carry forth in their congregations and other religious settings are also forms of ministry. But Ric's poetic/troubadour ministry had reached a certain level and had attained a certain kind of status in a way that called out for validation, at the professional level, by the

UUA itself. As Rev. Robert Swain, now in retirement, recalls: "I didn't originate the idea but I was on the UUA Board when the notion came up of granting Ric Ministerial Fellowship. As one of the few clergy there (on the Board), I was a major promoter of the idea that Ric already was a Unitarian Universalist minister—with the biggest parish on the continent—and it was high time we recognized that fact with credentials."

Part of Ric's decision to pursue the UU ministry came out of his conversations with Howard Matson. At about the same time that Ric was thinking of petitioning for the UU ministry Howard was planning to leave his position with the San Francisco UU Church to work with Caesar Chavez in creating a ministry to and with migrant farmers. As Rosemary remembers it, "Up to that point everything had been parish ministry. There was no kind of community ministry that anyone had ever heard of. Then Howard began talking about a migrant ministry, as something other than parish. From Howard's move Ric then got the idea that he wanted to be a troubadour minister. The two of them were the UUA's first community ministers before we started calling it that."

For Ric, the decision had an intensely personal element to it above and beyond the institutional reasons: "This is a very personal thing. I was learning disabled—dyslectic—and I had no degree. But the UUA still decided to sponsor me to tour their churches and campus sites using a fund that was aimed at sponsoring UUs to speak in academic settings. I decided I was doing a job of ministry. I'd been in churches and on college campuses for three years. I'm not a parish minister but I'd come in and tell the good news and people got excited and invigorated. I decided this was a form of ministry. But mainly I was trying to find out if I was OK. If the UU smart types could look at this singer who had flunked out of four colleges and dropped out of a fifth—well, in a way, being Fellowshipped was a way of graduating college."

Ric also feels that had he applied for Fellowship prior to merger, and solely with the Unitarians, he probably would have been denied access to the professional ministry. He was granted Fellowship by the UUA just ten years after the Unitarian and Universalist merger or consolidation. There was still some degree of institutional memory around from the Universalist tradition of the circuit riding Universalist minister, whose formal education may have been limited, but who performed a very effective and necessary ministry nonetheless. This Universalist circuit rider ministry is the tradition out of which Ric sees his own UU ministry. In his words, "I'm a Universalist Unitarian. I'm closer to the Universalist tradition of being out in the country, moving around and meeting people and helping them raise barns, than I am to the Unitarian tradition of being deep thinkers in and around the environs of Boston."

With the backing of Rosemary and Howard Matson, Ron Cook, and his Monterey parish minister Rev. Robert O'Brien, Ric did get his hearing before the Ministerial Fellowship Committee. Ron Cook recounts that the MFC didn't really know what, or who, they had on their hands, this candidate for the ministry with no seminary education or any other of the usual ministerial credentials. Harry Scholefield, who was the Senior Minister at the San Francisco UU Church had, at Howard Matson's request, come down to Big Sur and spent several days giving Ric a crash course tutorial on UU history and polity.

Ric was already so well traveled in UU circles, even after only 3-4 years, that he knew most of the ministers who were on the Committee at that time. But he still was not quite sure how to approach them. Being a little uncharacteristically cautious, he decided to play it straight by not playing or singing anything. He left his trademark guitar at home. The process for a ministerial candidate before the MFC is that s/he prepares and delivers a 10-15 minute sermon for the Committee, and then submits to the Committee's questions. So, playing it straight, Ric prepared and delivered a sermon which incorporated some of his poems.

The only thing Ric says he remembers about what followed is a tongue lashing he got from Rev. Renford Gaines, who later would take the name of Mwalimu Imara. Ric and Gaines/Imara already knew each other from Ric's being on the circuit and had become friends. But that didn't stop Rev. Imara from giving Ric a good blasting: "What do you think you're doing here like this!? Are you trying to play some kind of game with this Committee!? Where are your tools, man!? You haven't even shown us your tools for ministry!?..." And on like that until, as Ric remembers, "There was nothing but silence in the room and I felt wrung out." But Ric also recalls, "When I talked to him (Imara) later he said 'I hoped you could see the gleam in my eye that said I love you, I love you...'"

With the clarity of 20/20 hindsight Ric saw that Mwalimu was taking him to task for not offering the Committee his most authentic self. The missing tools Rev. Imara was referring to were Ric's absent guitar, his usually unorganized sheaf of poems, and his general fly-by-the-seat-of-the-pants way of being before a group of people. In Rev. Imara's eyes Ric was trying to join the MFC's dance instead of doing his own.

The only other thing Ric remembers is, "He (Imara) had beat the hell out of me so badly that nobody else had anything to say except for a couple of little questions. I went outside thinking that I didn't have a prayer. Then Carl Scovel came through the door and said, 'I want you to know that you have been Fellowshipped by a 100% vote; and this is such an important occasion that I want to book you for an appearance at King's Chapel.'"

The only stipulation that the MFC put on Ric's ministerial credentials was that he would never put his name forward for settlement in a UU parish ministry setting unless he first went to seminary for two years. This is an agreement that Ric has not come close to violating in all the years that have gone by since that day in 1971.

The following summer, at the General Assembly in Washington, D.C., Ric was formally ordained to the UU ministry by the Unitarian Universalist Church of Arlington, Virginia. Their Associate Minister at the time, Rev. George Pete Tolleson, who had become one of Ric's good friends, led the service. Ric recalls: "There was a huge crowd. I did a short concert and then Pete, representing the Arlington UU Church, did the honors, and loaves of bread were passed around for communion."

The final come-round-again part of this story occurred five years later when Ric was recognized for Final Fellowship at the 1976 General Assembly, which was held on the campus of Pomona College in Claremont, California. It was a very emotional moment for him: "As it turned out the first college I flunked out of was Pomona College, and that's where the GA was held the year I got my Final Fellowship. I walked across the stage where I would have walked across years earlier had I managed to graduate from college. It was just one of those synchronistic things. I wept like a baby."

CHAPTER THREE:

The Minister/Poet—How Exposed and Vulnerable?

the cup looked half empty
the big hand said forty-two past
and the word if there was one
was "tired"

then suddenly the wind touched my hair
and I became aware of myself
there on the bridge
a weary old bird ready to leap
from the nest and fly blind
to the breathing sea below
me in my best bulky-knit sweater
calmly inching forward a great sadness
in my blue-gray eyes—hair blowing
aware now I paused and listened
to the night for motor sound
and looked for lights
but the world was empty
no one was coming to witness
my final scene—the grand finale

*and it was such a fantastic
dramatic moment I decided
to came back and tell you all about it
laughing—shaking my head*

*I drove home but it wasn't
until I saw the shape of my own house
that I discovered the cup
had been half full all the time*

*I was told recently
that of all witnessed suicides
from the Golden Gate Bridge
in San Francisco, California
not one—not a single person
has been seen to go off
on the ocean side—the horizon side
all—as of this writing have been seen
leaping back toward the city
and that would be a hell of a thing
to discover half way down*

*once years ago I hung by my heels
was swatted—whaaaaaah!
and decided to suck air and live
--on a bridge near Big Sur, California
in the summer of '71
I faced the same decision again
and as I write this
I realize I am three months old today*

The Bixby Bridge Incident by Ric Masten

In the *Rainbow Zen* poem that led off the first chapter of this book Ric Masten makes reference to having "read Sartrees and Camoose." In his perusing of "Camoose" maybe he read the opening lines to Albert Camus's *The Myth of Sisyphus* where the French existentialist philosopher and playwright states, "There is but one truly serious philosophical problem, and that is suicide. Judging whether life is or is not worth living amounts to answering the fundamental question of philosophy. All the rest…comes afterwards."

For Ric it was less philosophical speculation and more tiredness and feelings of being burned out that brought him to his "Camoose moment," and led him to drive a few miles south of the intersection of California's Highway One and Palo Colorado Road to the Bixby Bridge in the summer of 1971. Even with his being granted UU ministerial status, and making a well established name for himself within and well beyond UU circles, there was also a worn and prone to depression side of the Rev. Masten that would still show itself from time to time. It was this side that got him to the bridge.

The Bixby Bridge is a breathtaking engineering marvel as it spans the mouth of Big Sur's Bixby Canyon and Creek with a seemingly endless Pacific Ocean off to the west. This bridge provided Jack Kerouac the central image for his novel *Big Sur*. It is a very, very long way down from the bridge's railing to the beach below. If one is looking for a permanent exit, a leap off the Bixby Bridge is a sure road out. But, as his poem tells it, in Ric's case it turned out to be a road not taken.

As Ric set out for another round of troubadour ministry following the summer of '71, this poem, in certain locales, became added to his set. He also worked in a few others that showed his more vulnerable, needful, and even painful side. For all of the freedom, promise, hope and joy the road offers, it can also bring a pronounced measure of weariness, sadness and despair. Maybe Ric was meeting the shadow side of himself on the shadow side of his road, while still being able to gently mock himself that "no one was coming to witness my final scene, the grand finale."

If there's a counter-point to *The Bixby Bridge Incident*, it would be one of the trademark songs that characterized the mood and tone of Ric's early road appearances called

CHRISTOPHER SUNSHINE

Once a young hitch-hiker stepped inside my car
Said: I am Christopher Sunshine
And I have traveled far
An' I got things to tell you, gifts that I will give
I am Christopher Sunshine and I have learned to live...

An' I felt a feelin' of freedom lift this ol' heart of mine.
And when he got out at the crossroads
He left a rose behind
And that's what Christopher Sunshine gave me as a gift
Then he put his thumb out
And caught another lift.

Such had been—and still is—the usual flavor of a Ric Masten appearance. He travels in from afar, shares his message, gives his gifts of joy and hope, leaves a rose behind, and then catches another lift out of town. But what happens when Christopher Sunshine gets the blues, or runs low on roses? Where does he go with his hurt? Indeed, this is one of the toughest questions a minister faces. S/he is certainly not expected to constantly maintain a feel-good façade, but there is a "minister mode" in which members of the clergy need to operate if they are to be effective. How much latitude can and should a minister have within that mode when it comes to being vulnerable, and showing his/her needy and hurting side to the congregation, or whatever constituency it is, that s/he serves? Concerns in the early stages of his ministry that Ric was crossing a line by exposing his vulnerability nearly cost him his ministerial standing with the Unitarian Universalists.

An early warning for Ric came in the form of a four page single-spaced letter to him from Rev. Glenn Turner in December of 1971 after some of his appearances in the Pacific Northwest. Glenn was serving the Tacoma, Washington UU Church and had become a good friend and strong advocate for Ric as he'd been the agent for some of his Billings appearances in that region. On this round of gigs Ric had read the Bixby Bridge poem along with a few others that revealed his more hurting side. Taken as a whole the letter reflects Glenn's love and concern for Ric; but Glenn pulls no punches either: [Note: The copies of the Turner/Masten letters that were made available to me have numerous names and places excised.]

"The first thing you greeted ****** with was the 'bridge' experience. The suicide references did turn people off. Your 'ministry' is a kind of sharing of your 'misery'. It's not the good news of the gospel according to Christopher Sunshine. Ric, can you draw a line between a performer and a human being? Can you imagine that you can do a good thing for people in one place and that you can get the hurts healed somewhere else? I don't feel it's fair to you or our churches to send (out) a dejected troubadour who hasn't gone through some Easter trip yet." Tough stuff! But it was also tough love.

Of course, Ric had his right of reply which he exercised in a four page response. Much of Ric's letter addressed an age old dilemma that ministers and their congregations face. If being a minister, especially when in the pulpit and before a congregation, is more than being an entertainer who makes people happy, then what does the "more than entertainer" part consist of? This, as Ric described it to Glenn, was the issue he was struggling with. He was being billed as an entertainer when he wanted to be a minister. Whatever errors in judgment Ric made (and which he acknowledged) were ones he made in the course of trying to differentiate between the two. As he put it: "Christopher Sunshine is a half truth that must be balanced by the 'there ain't no Santa Claus' poem, which is also a half truth which needs an equal amount of Christopher Sunshine. If I was short on Christopher

Sunshine in ***** that night then I'm sorry." He continues: "If I must be the carefree Hollywood dropout who moved to magic mountain making adroit comments to the beat of a big guitar, I would be presenting a ghastly lie, a false hope. I've been trying to make meaning, not give answers."

As for his lack of an Easter experience Ric answered with this: "Now look at the last line of the (Bixby Bridge) poem: 'and as I write this I realize that I am three months old today.' If this isn't Easter and rebirth then I don't know what is. If I did not make that clear in ***** then I really did blow it. I was standing there in front of the group saying I'd found a reason to live, and that while I would have to pay a price for my sunflowers, that was OK because we have time for much joy before we go over the falls."

The issue here, to be sure, is not who was "right" and who was "wrong." Ric and Glenn were trying to meet each other with their most authentic and honest selves. Glenn was trying to get Ric to appreciate the distinction—granted an often fuzzy one—between his public minister self and his warts-and-all self. Ric was trying to get beyond the traveling minister as entertainer role he felt he was largely being cast in, and trapped in.

In fact it was the *Bixby Bridge Incident* poem, as Ric looks back on it, that helped to provide a structure for his appearances, particularly in church settings. He came to arrange his performance poems in thirds: "The first third would be 'Christmas.' It would just have to do with birth and life—funny stuff as well as my social action stuff. Then one third would be 'Good Friday' poems that would deal with death and depression and the shadow side of life. The final third would be 'Easter,' dealing with resurrection motifs and affirming that life was worth living. When I'd do it that way people had automatically had communion."

Looking back on the original incident some 35 years later Glenn Tuner reflects, "You had times when his (Ric's) behaviors may have hurt others. But I'm not a therapist, and I'm not sure I really got through well enough to say what I actually meant. I wasn't really mature enough at the time." Glenn goes on, "But can you judge a poet that way—as you would others? We (Ric and I) really are friends and have a way of caring about each other."

With his comment "Can you judge a poet that way?" Glenn put his finger on the tantalizing dilemma of assessing Ric Masten as a minister when he's also a poet. The minister piece and the poet piece of his life are difficult, if not impossible, to separate. But each piece has its distinctive roles and demands. A poet stands naked before his or her listeners and readers; a minister is expected to have at least a few pieces of clothing on. What do you do when you're both? That was the issue behind the issue of the Turner/Masten letters.

Nearly three years after they were written these letters played a crucial role in determining whether or not Ric would receive Final Fellowship in the UU ministry. There was still enough concern around about his use of the "suicide poem" that it became an issue when Ric came up for his Final Fellowship with the Ministerial Fellowship Committee. The Fellowshipping process in the UUA happens in two steps. One is first granted Preliminary Fellowship for a minimum period of three years which is something of a probationary time. Final Fellowship is granted based on the minister's performance and general aptitude during the Preliminary phase. The minister does not usually appear before the MFC when being considered for Final Fellowship.

John Buehrens, who would eventually become President of the UUA, was in his second year as a student at the Harvard Divinity School, and served on the MFC at that time as their student representative. He and Ric had already become friends. John recalls both the initial rationale for granting Ric Preliminary Fellowship, and how the issue came to be raised again when his time for Final Fellowship came around, with the Bixby Bridge poem hovering over that decision.

As for the Preliminary Fellowship decision, John's account speaks to the issue noted in the previous chapter: "Ric was given Preliminary Fellowship with the specialized ministry category. He told the MFC that he'd become a UU ambassador in their churches and that was he was doing was ministry and should be acknowledged as such. He was representing UUism in a public way. He told them, in effect, either I'm doing a ministry for you guys and I should be acknowledged as a minister, or your churches are so darned dull that you need to hire an entertainer! [Note: This is Buehrens characterization and not Ric's words.] The MFC decided they'd rather call him a minister than a hired entertainer. I was sympathetic to that point of view."

Buehrens picks up the story when the time to grant, or not grant, Ric Final Fellowship came around: "I was the student minister on the MFC for their Boston meetings. In the first gathering of the Committee it became clear that Rev. Alan Deale, who was an MFC member, was mad as hell at Ric over the suicide poem. Ric had been in Portland, Oregon, where Alan was the minister, a few years earlier and had entertained the children with the *Dirty Word Song* and *Let It Be A Dance.* A fine time was had by all and everything was breezy. Then he came back a year later and did his 'Shall I throw myself from the bridge?' stuff. He did it on a Sunday morning at Alan's church with kids present. I had to admit it was probably a lapse in judgment, what with kids there. But it was also clear to me that since Ric was in Preliminary Fellowship they were just going to terminate his Fellowship and re-think this whole business of specialized ministries. The MFC at the time was dominated by senior male ministers. There was only one female minister on the Committee."

John continues: "I decided this wasn't fair and that Ric should have a hearing. I knew he was touring in New England so I went home and got ahold of him and essentially said, 'Ric, I don't care how you do it but day after tomorrow you need to be in Boston; and tomorrow you have to call the Department of Ministry and demand to be heard before the MFC. Otherwise you're cooked.' He did get up there and had an interview with the Committee. I think by then the MFC was too tired to take any drastic action. So they said alright we'll keep you in, but watch it!"

Ric's recollection of the matter is that he knew the issue had arisen, and he had sent the Committee copies of the letters he and Glenn Turner had exchanged to demonstrate both his awareness of the matter at hand, and his perspective on it. When he got before the Committee he asked them if they had read his letter. None of them, according to Ric, had. So he asked that they read the letter and read the poem, and particularly look at the poem's outcome with its theme of rebirth. This apparently carried the day for him. Ric's take on the matter is, "If I hadn't gone and defended myself I probably would have lost my standing as a minister…(but) Alan Deale and I have remained friends. When I got my Final Fellowship Alan was there to give me a big hug when I came across the stage."

While the question of whether or not Ric Masten would remain in the UU ministry was settled several decades ago, the larger issue behind *The Bixby Bridge Incident* is one that ministers, especially those in the parish, continually have to deal with and continually have to revisit. A minister in an ongoing settlement has to deal with the needs and expectations that the congregation—consciously or not—projects onto him or her. A minister is expected to represent a faith tradition as well as be the local embodiment of that tradition in serving a congregation. On top of all that, this man or woman is also supposed to be a human being with all that one's humanity encompasses. One of the many balancing acts a minister has to maintain lies in having a congregation who wants to know that their minister is a human being, and who bleeds when wounded—but they still don't want their minister bleeding all over them! Nor, in fairness, should they have to. A congregation is not their minister's personal therapist.

Ric gained an appreciation of this ministerial dilemma when singing another of his shadow-side poems at a party. The song/poem is *To Stevie: From the Shore*. It is Ric's reply to a poem by the British poet Stevie Smith called *Drowning, Not Waving*. Here are a couple of verses:

I ain't wavin' babe,
I'm drownin'
Goin' down in a cold, lonely sea
I ain't wavin' babe
I'm drown'
So babe quit wavin' at me

This ain't singin' babe
This here's screamin'
I'm screamin' that I'm gonna drown.
And you're smilin' babe
And you're wavin'
Just like you don't hear a sound…

Hey babe, are you drownin' too?
Oh babe, you're drownin' too.
Oh

Ric recalls being at a party with Howard and Rosemary Matson, where several members of the congregation Howard was serving at the time were also present. Part of the reason for having the party was so Ric could sing some of his songs for the gathering. Along with the mostly upbeat and breezy (Christmas) ones he did he also threw in a little Good Friday by singing *From the Shore*. When Ric was finished, Howard remarked to a woman, a member of his congregation named Phyllis, how much he liked *From the Shore*. Phyllis' response was, "Howard, I do not want my minister to tell me he's drowning!" Ric quickly came to see that while Phyllis liked his song, and liked the way he sang it, she still did not want "my minister," in this case the Rev. Howard Matson, relating to it all that closely!

Reflecting on this Ric acknowledges, "I could bring certain things up because I'd be leaving town the next day. The settled minister would still be there and couldn't do that. Part of my value was to come in in a very personal way—which is what poetry is, very personal—and bring up a lot of subjects that would be very hard for a minister to be personal about."

By offering an alternative, and very short-term type of ministry, Ric was offering a service to our congregations that the settled minister was not nearly as well positioned to do. Ric was better positioned to expose some of his vulnerabilities, which in turn could, and often did, offer an invitation to his listeners to confront some of the unhealed parts of themselves as well. He performed a real pastoral service in this regard. In so doing, of course, he also ran the risk of crossing a line, or getting a bit out of bounds now and then, even for a poet/troubadour minister. But, then, ministry of any kind has always been a very risky business!

There is one more related matter to be explored here which has to do with a minister's ego needs and how they get met. It is closely tied to the issue of a minister's vulnerabilities and how much exposure they should be given. Parts of this chapter have attempted to deal with the differentiation between performer, entertainer, and minister. Such differentiations can and must be made. But the lines between these categories do not break cleanly. Along with being a minister, poet, and philosopher of a sort, Ric Masten *is* also a performer and an entertainer, which in turn calls upon him to be a self-promoter. But isn't this the case—provided they're really honest about it—with practically all ministers? Perhaps the Rev. Ric Masten has simply been more overt in his performing, entertaining, and self-promoting ways, while the great majority of the clergy—especially those in Unitarian Universalist and mainline Protestant circles—have to be more subtle about it.

A verse from Ric's poem *Notice Me!* will move us along here:

> *put me in your human eye*
> *come taste the bitter tears that i cry*
> *touch me with your human hand*
> *hear me with your ear*

and notice me!
damn you—notice me
I'm here

To put these words in their original, and intended, context Ric is actually assuming the voice of one of his young daughters in this poem as she asks for her father's attention, while her father is too immersed in his career pursuits to adequately offer it. We'll revisit this poem in the chapter on "Family Matters." Like a lot of poetry, however, this one can be read on several levels beyond the poet's original intent. Somewhere in their heart of hearts, whether consciously or not, ministers say much of these same words to those whom they try to serve: "touch me with your human hand…hear me with your ear…and notice me! damn you—notice me…I'm here."

Yes, we say we do it for God, or for a faith tradition, or for humanity, or because we want to give of ourselves, or for dozens of other such reasons. We're not lying to ourselves, or to anyone else, in so doing and thinking; not at all. I marvel, in fact, at the tremendous sacrifices of time and money and career and family that so many women and men make these days just to gain entry into the professional ministry. But to speak of the call to ministry in entirely selfless terms is to be less than honest as well. Somewhere in the soul of the one who hears that call, in all of its authenticity, is the Coffee Table Dancer who wants to be noticed and touched and heard.

Any good minister knows that the ministry is not the entertainment business, but still wishes—at least at times—to be entertaining. We want to hear a good laugh from the congregation when we put out a line that is supposed to get one. A good minister knows that leading a worship service and preaching is not supposed to be a performance, in the sense of something that is artificially staged; but to provide a meaningful worship experience one has to be something of a performer nonetheless.

Consider also that a minister in the Unitarian Universalist and mainline Protestant tradition delivers, on average, some 35-40 sermons a year. There's a certain amount of chutzpa involved in thinking we've got something worthwhile to say, and worthy of being heard, that many times a year by a roomful of people! And yet we—most of us anyway—put our sermon titles in our newsletters and in our local newspapers, expecting people to show up and hear what we have to say. For all of our rationales about "getting our message out" is there not at least some degree of self-promotion going on here? If so, is that really such a bad thing? If Rev. Robert O'Brien had not seen fit to publicize the fact in a Monterey newspaper that he was going to deliver a sermon on the topic of *Are We Actors or Authors?* the chances are pretty good that a book about Ric Masten, Unitarian Universalist minister, would never be written.

One of the more crucial challenges a parish minister faces, and which the members of the congregation need to appreciate is how to acknowledge that minister's ego needs while not allowing those needs to define or dominate his or her ministry. Anyone entering the ministry is immediately placed on a steep learning curve about how to best accomplish this balancing act in ways that will enhance, and not destroy, the ministry itself. A congregation who calls a minister to his or her first settlement needs to be especially sensitive to this.

In Ric Masten's early years as a UU minister, poet, and troubadour he was on a similar kind of learning curve even though he was not serving in a parish setting. He had to struggle with some of the same issues that settled ministers do, especially in the early years of their ministries: How open can I be with some of my own demons while also trying to bring a healing voice and presence to those with whom I minister? How do I deal with my own need to be noticed when a major part of my calling is to notice others? When I stand before a congregation how do I balance my being an entertainer and a performer with the expectations of those before me that I speak words of wisdom, power, and transformation?

With his troubadour style of ministry Ric could deal with these questions and issues in a more quick, overt and direct way than can the minister who is still going to be around for another day or year or decade. And for whatever eyebrows he may have raised in the process, and for whatever lines he may have occasionally crossed, Ric in his more vulnerable moments was also rendering a service to clergy and laity alike by pointing to some of the deepest and most difficult challenges those who respond to the call of ministry face.

He may have only been a second year divinity school student at the time, and while he went on to serve our liberal religious movement in many exemplary ways, one of the greatest services John Buehrens may have performed for our Association was the role he played in saving Ric Masten's ministry while it was still getting off the ground. The loss of such a ministry as Ric's would have been a sad one indeed. Instead we can rejoice in the life that his ministry has had.

CHAPTER FOUR:

The Minister/Poet—As Pastor

he rode a pale white horse—away
for he was twenty six
O.D.'d
killed himself with heroin
and although I didn't know him
I am a minister
so I said this at his memorial service

first
I said his name
and then I said he was old enough to say
I am
and so he was
the proof of it gathered before me
in them
who had known him first hand
in them
who were more than they might have been
because of his being

again I said his name
and then I said
that even I who had never met him

had met him there
in them that day

a pebble does not

enter a pond without
    a
 ripple
 moving out
and in time touching
every single shore—we are all
every one of us in this thing together

again said his name
and then I said that he had been
this was certain
and he having been must always be

   nothing is lost
   nothing is wasted
   no one
    none of us
     not one of us
     is that
alone

***A Minister* by Ric Masten**

"Although I didn't know him I am a minister…" I doubt there's a minister alive who cannot in some way relate to the story Ric tells in this poem. Maybe not the specifics, but getting a call from a funeral director, or a friend of a friend, or from someone who has somehow heard good things about you, and asking if you'd lead a memorial service—this is a story about which practically every minister can tell his or her version. Some of the more meaningful funeral or memorial services I've led are ones where I didn't know the deceased, and yet had that person's family and friends open up to me about their feelings for the one they'd lost in some truly amazing ways.

The story Ric tells with this poem is also something of a microcosm for the pastoral piece of his troubadour ministry. In many instances his was pastoral care done on the run and on the road. It was done while standing before, and conversing with, people he scarcely knew. This is not the way the pastoral side of ministry is accomplished in more traditional ministerial settings. Pastoral ministry usually grows out of the relationships a minister develops with members of his/her congregation. It grows out of the trust that is formed in such relationships. It is when a congregant comes to feel that the minister is someone s/he feels secure and trusting enough to be open with that pastoral ministry takes place.

But there are also persons who seem to have a gift for establishing an almost instant rapport with those whom they encounter, which in turn very quickly creates surprising levels of openness. To possess such a gift is both a wonderful and precarious thing, for it is a gift that can be used for great good or for great harm. When the Unitarian Universalists made Ric their troubadour minister they were entrusting him with his gift of poetic self-disclosure, which could in turn very quickly generate significant levels of self-disclosure on the part of his listeners and hearers. The concerns some of those on the Ministerial Fellowship Committee had about Ric's use of his "suicide poem" (as told in Chapter Three) were about how well, or not, Ric was using this gift of his. He may have got a little close to the line with that one, but that poem has had a number of positive pastoral outcomes over the years.

When Rosemary Matson, Ric and Billie's friend and fellow UU for over 40 years, was asked what she felt Ric's most important contribution to Unitarian Universalism has been, she offered this: "By being open about himself, Ric has opened up a lot of other people who otherwise would not have been. He opened people up by talking about his problems as personal examples. When he was first on the scene it was embarrassing, sometimes, for some people to hear him. But by showing the value of being open and honest about oneself, he encouraged others to do so."

Among the earliest expressions of the pastoral side of Ric's ministry was his ability to connect with certain elements of the youth culture of the late 1960s and early 70s. The mantra for that culture, and that era, was "you can't trust anyone over 30." But here was an "elder" in his late 30s, moving into his 40s, who was deemed trustworthy. Following his introduction to the wider UU family at the 1968 General Assembly Ric was made a UU ambassador with the task, as John Buehrens put it, "of taking the spirit of liberal religion to college campuses about the country." As already noted, religious bodies of various stripes have long been bedeviled by the challenge of reaching the youth and young adult population from their late teens to their late 20s. Ric Masten, by and large, represented the Unitarian Universalist's attempt to respond to this challenge in the era being cited here. And for a time he did have something of an *ad hoc* youth ministry program going in and out of his Palo Colorado Canyon home.

The starting point for this ministry was the annual summer gathering of Central Pacific UUs at a conference center in Asilomar, California in 1969. Asilomar is a small coastal enclave next to Pacific Grove; and is less than an hour's drive from the Masten's home. Ric was invited as one of the resource people to that year's Asilomar gathering, largely because he was not Ken Kesey. The year before, 1968, Ken Kesey and his Merry Pranksters had been the invited guests at Asilomar and had managed to wreak a certain amount of havoc on the gathering by pushing the UU's liberal boundaries well beyond their comfort level—which was what Kesey, with a method to his madness approach, was deliberately trying to do. I refer those readers who would like to know that story to the chapter titled "A Miracle in Seven Days" in Tom Wolfe's *The Electric Kool-Aid Acid Test*.

In the aftershocks of the Kesey/Merry Pranksters appearance, the UU conference planners for the following year decided they still needed someone who was relatively hip, and to whom the youth contingent in attendance could hopefully relate, but who wouldn't be squirreling their kids away in a Day-Glo painted bus! Their solution was Ric Masten, who described himself as a "Beatie"—that is, someone between a Beat and a Hippie. It was a good call all the way around, and it marked the beginning of Ric's bead ministry.

Some weeks before the conference one of Ric's neighbors, who was part of a hippie influx into Palo Colorado Canyon, caught him in what she recognized as a down moment. Ric was battling the flu. The woman was Helen Weston, the ex-wife of photographer, Cole Weston. Helen gave Ric her string of beads, saying "you look like you could use these more than I need them." Ric wore the beads to Asilomar, at which point they took on a life of their own:

"So I had this conference coming up and I'd just gotten my beads. My first hippie beads! I got to talking to somebody there—one of the congregants at Asilomar, the one after Kesey—and her story was so sad that I just sort of instinctively put the beads on her and said, 'You can't keep these; you can only wear them as long as you need them, or until you run into somebody who needs them more than you do; and you have to give them with the same instructions.' Less than six hours later I see that my beads are being worn by someone else, and I first thought, 'Well, gee, here I had this wonderful moment and obviously it didn't mean that much to that person.' I thought she was treating my beads in an off-hand kind of way. Then I came to find out that the woman to whom the beads had been given had terminal cancer. The woman to whom I'd given the beads found someone who needed them more than she did. Those beads got passed around during that whole conference."

Ric even got a short poem out of this experience in which he takes a playful jab at himself:

THE MINISTER/POET—AS PASTOR

BEAD GAME

I have given gifts
Trinkets
Inexpensive tokens of my affection
But with instructions
That you must pass them on
Give them away
To someone you love and admire

And when you do
I am crushed

The story continues: "So the next year before I went back to Asilomar I paid my kids a dollar a string to make me some beads, and I'd go out and have these moments. I'd stress that you can't keep the beads, that they are a way of passing along some of the love and care that has been shown to you. I had a lot of bead moments after that."

In time however, those bead moments—which gave Ric a way of doing a pastoral ministry—began to lose their meaning for him. Here is yet another challenge of ministry: How do you keep it real when you're doing the same thing over a certain stretch of time? What happens when something that is losing its kick for you continues to have a lot of meaning for others? In Ric's words again:

"Those were real moments I was having, but at the same time it was becoming not as real for me. I'd put the beads on you and we'd have our moment and then you'd disappear around the corner. So after a couple of years of doing the beads here, there, and wherever I started to say 'this is phony Ric, you've got to stop.' It got to feeling so rote that I stopped doing it.

"But then I was asked back to a place I'd been before—Kennewick, Washington—and I stayed with the same family as when I'd been doing my beads. As soon as I arrived this young girl came running out to Ric Masten the minister and she put beads on me. I said, 'Thank you, but I'm really not into this anymore.' And she burst into tears and went to her room crying. I wondered what was going on. I was still learning my trade in those days."

When it comes to learning their trade, as Ric puts it, one of the more important things a minister has to learn is how to maintain his or her authenticity and freshness in dealing with people who want and need essentially the same things from their minister over the years. Ministry in all its many dimensions (pastoral and otherwise) can get stale for the minister even as it has to remain fresh for the congregants or for those with whom she or he ministers, whatever the setting. Even as a troubadour minister, Ric got a taste of this challenge in the episode he describes.

My own way of meeting this challenge—and sometimes I'm more successful at it than others—is to try to maintain the awareness that while ministry may be something that I do, it is not in the end about me. It is rather about how the components of my pastoral ministry, however rote they may come to seem to me at certain points, have their effect on others in ways that have nothing to do with my feelings. Practically any minister out there has a number of stories about how a near-forgotten deed of care and kindness, that may have seemed like no big deal at the time, comes back around for a visit, even from a distant past. To pick up on Ric's story again, here is one of the ways the effects of his bead ministry came full circle:

"In time the beads did get put away. Then just recently, since my cancer diagnosis (1999), I got this little bell in the mail. It came from a guy whose father, the Rev. Orloff Miller, had been a minister near Denver some 30 years ago. I went to see Orloff's son, Orloff Jr., in a hospital in Colorado Springs when he was a kid and was quite sick. His minister father asked me to pay him a visit. So I went and sang him a few songs and put some beads on the boy.

"The note that came with the bell was from Orloff, Jr. and it said, 'We LRYers (Liberal Religious Youth) fell in love with what you did with the beads. The ones you gave me got broken apart and then got restrung, and my LRY friends passed them around in Denver for a time. But I always kept the bell you gave me with the beads. Then I read about you on line [about getting cancer] and figured you needed them back.' My own beads, coming back to me!"

Such is the nature of a well done pastoral ministry. It can come back to you in ways you'll never anticipate. Rev. Robert Swain offers yet another example of the enduring effect of a small deed of kindness and caring—this one directed at his three year old daughter: "In 1968 Ric won the undying love and admiration of my 3-year-old daughter, Rachel, when he took her aside one afternoon (after she was showing signs of being upset that the three adults were having a great time while she was being left out) and he sang *The Dirty Word Song* and a few others just for her in another room. I'm sure lots of other tots got similar treatment, and I'm sure they all likewise have a warm spot in their heart for our beloved troubadour."

To return for a few moments to where the bead ministry story began, it was the Asilomar conference that kicked off a spontaneous kind of youth ministry that Ric carried out for a few years thereafter. His home became a stopping off, crash pad place for many of the young on-the-roaders of that time. Ric again: "Asilomar was a difficult conference. I was supposed to be the youth counselor. People thought I was going to be another Ken Kesey but I wasn't. I was only giving beads away, not drugs. Well, that conference started the hippie treks to my place. Here I was this old guy in his forties doing this song called *Drop Out*. We had kids camping out around here, just like they used to go to Henry Miller's place a few more miles down the coast. But in time it got to be too much and Billie finally said no more. This has to stop. These kids can't be here all the time."

The treks may have stopped, but there are still plenty of people around—now in their fifties and early sixties—who remember finding a safe haven and a sympathetic ear atop Palo Colorado Canyon while they were searching for the paths their lives would eventually take.

And while Ric had a way of meaningfully connecting with the youth culture of the late 60s and early 70s, he did not romanticize it. He was also able to see the self-indulgent and unduly self-possessed side of that culture as well, as this story indicates:

"I was here the day the music died. It was at the time of the Monterey Pop festival. This canyon was full. It was a hippie Mecca. And alongside the road there at the bottom of Murray Grade was an old cabin. It had been there for about ten years and hikers used it. The idea was that if you used it you were to leave it in a little better shape than you found it—do a little repair, fix it up in even some small way. So the Monterey Pop was over and Billie and I went for a walk. We came by the cabin. The roof had caved in. We went in and saw that the kids who had come to see the rock fest had torn the inside wall down to build a fire that night. All over the floor was expensive silverware. I said, 'God, it's over. These are user kids.' They were upper middle class kids who had come to hear a rock festival and do their week-end hippie thing. They trashed a cabin instead of leaving it in better shape for the next visitors. And I thought, Goddamn, it's died."

Those days were both a wonderful and an exceedingly difficult and painful time to be in the liberal ministry in America in any kind of setting. Ric Masten wore the mantle of a UU minister well during that era. Rev. Mwalimu Imara (nee Renford Gaines), who had chided Ric about his lack of tools at his Ministerial Fellowship Committee hearing, pays him this tribute that well sums up his ministry of that time: "I do remember Ric singing at my home and at church. I'll always remember him as a troubadour of love and sanity during insane times."

Ric's ministry—pastoral and otherwise—hardly ended as the 1970s wound down. It may not have had as high a profile as in its earlier and headier days, but his ministry continued to touch many lives very deeply on many personal levels. There are any number of stories that could be offered about how Ric's troubadour ministry of love and sanity, as Rev. Imara calls it, has played out over the years and decades.

This is one by Dr. John Frykman of San Francisco, a minister with the American Lutheran Church. Dr. Frykman tells of how his relationship with Ric began under quite humorous circumstances, and then deepened over the years:

"Sometime in the early 70s I was waiting in line at Boston's Logan Airport to get my seat assignment for a flight to San Francisco and then Monterey. I heard a voice say, 'John, how about we get a seat together. It's time we got to know each other. I'm Ric Masten.' I knew three of Ric's children through some of the work I'd done in the schools in Monterey, but he and I had never met. It was such a coincidence that we met in the heart of Unitarian Universalist country—I who had worked as a janitor in a Universalist Church in Philadelphia while attending Lutheran Theological Seminary and Ric the emerging troubadour for the UUA.

"We boarded the flight and the pilot came on and perfectly mimicked Lyndon Johnson as he described the flight plan. Ric and I looked at each other and laughed, 'What a perfect imitation of LBJ—he's got to be kidding!' So we sent a note up to the pilot commending him on his impersonation. He came back on the PA, this time imitating Jimmy Stewart, and said, 'Well, at least two of you appreciate what I'm doing.' And then he invited us to move up to First Class for the remainder of the flight! It was one of those moments made in heaven. We luxuriated: Free booze, fine food, lots of attention, and six hours to get to know each other."

Out of this meet-up Ric found himself recruited as a troubadour minister to the Lutherans for a time: "He (Frykman) got me to do an Asilomar thing for the Lutherans. I even went on a Lutheran tour. The interesting thing is that they were absolutely no different from the UUs in their homes and churches. A minister is a minister." Due to his Lutheran appearances, and his connection to Rev. Frykman, *Let It Be A Dance* was included in a Lutheran hymnal.

Frykman goes on to tell of how the relationship between him and Ric deepened and grew over the years following their chance encounter:

"I have no way of knowing how many times we have seen or been with each other over the years since then. There have been workshops and family interactions. Ric and Billie Barbara came to one of my wife's and my renewal parties. We do a renewal arrangement of our marriage every year like he and Billie do [See the *Family Matters* chapter]. We've seen one another through dark valleys, like teachers and students being killed in a car crash [Described in the *Minister as Theologian* chapter]. A mutual friend killed himself and Ric handled the funeral. He's had his own dark valleys of despair and I've gone to share them with him."

Frykman concludes:

"The amazing thing is, when we see each other once again, it's like no time has passed. One and a half years ago (2004) we did a retreat for an Episcopal Church group. It was like we had been doing it all along, over and over, even though it was the first time we'd ever done such an event together. As one of Ric's poems puts it, 'We all will do what we must do, simply to exist.'"

The reference to a mutual friend committing suicide and Ric doing the funeral has overtones of the poem, *A Minister*, that opens this chapter, although in that poem and instance Ric did not know the deceased. Upon reading Dr. Frykman's thoughts about Ric, his son Lars weighed in with some accompanying thoughts of his own:

"When I was studying photography Ric gave me a copy of his book *Stark Naked*. The inscription he wrote for me said, 'For Lars, look up and live (pp. 35-44).' These pages contain photographs taken by the Westons [Cole, Kim, & Edward], who are very well known in the photography world, with poems written for and about them by Ric. Every now and then when I'm feeling down, sometimes I'll pick up this book and just open it to a random page to see what Ric has to say about my situation. It's pretty amazing how just so right on some of the things said in that book have been for me at any given 'random' moment in my life."

Lars then moved to the same incident as mentioned by his father:

THE MINISTER/POET—AS PASTOR

"The most beautiful moment I've had with that book came when a mutual friend of ours committed suicide. In my despair I went to that old friend of mine [the "friend" being Ric's book] and, I kid you not, randomly opened to page 44. On that page is a beautiful picture of Ric and his friend Cole in an embrace titled 'Friends.' The poem under the picture was/is perfect. I faxed it over to my father and told him to take it to the memorial service. It tore him up, and he agreed that it was perfect. Ric read that poem at the service for our friend."

Lars ends on this note:

"Ric gave me that book way back in 1981. I can't tell you how many times I've opened it up and laughed, cried, railed, and cheered with it. Funny how such a random act of kindness can turn into such a wonderful thing, but…that's Ric."

Among the many acts of kindness and inspiration that Ric and Billie Barbara have offered were the ones they brought to British Unitarians on a trip they made on behalf of the British Unitarian Council. Ric tells it this way: "I did a trip to England when Bob West was UUA President. Ron Cook took Billie and me there. I found the situation with the British Unitarian Church pretty sad at the time. I went to this church where there were twenty old women in attendance. They were the wives of guys who were killed in World War II. They seemed very stiff and I figured I'd never connect. But I went and did my gig, and they took out their hankies and laughed and cried loudly. I was really surprised. So I asked the local minister about their reaction. He told me, 'England is a pretty small island. We keep ourselves pretty straight-laced. The only place where we can let it go is in the theater, where we can laugh and cry as a bunch. You come into our churches as more theater than minister, so they can laugh and cry as if they are in a theater instead of a church.'"

For Billie the trip had a personal dimension of its own: "One of the highlights of my life was the trip we took to England. We went to Bolton. Bolton is my last name, and this is where my people came from. I felt like I'd come home."

After four decades of pastoral ministry on the road, the latest incarnation of Ric's ministry is now carried forth by way of his website. He calls those he reaches through this medium his cybergation: "My cybergation is also a ministry. There are some 2000 people to whom I send out my weekly *Words and One Liners*. I don't know if they're rich or poor, or what their gender or race or sexual orientation is. Whatever I post people can relate to, or take offense at, or respond to in some way. I guess it's a little like standing at the door after doing a sermon and greeting the people who have heard it as they leave the church. In my case I get about 50-70 replies a week from my cybergation out of the 600 or so hits I get. There are about ten people I hear from on a regular and ongoing basis. This is a ministry; a unique ministry. You meet people's spirits and minds. That's ministry."

Indeed it is. This meeting of people's spirits and minds is the kind of ministry Ric has been carrying forth now for close to 40 years. As will be seen in a later chapter, one of the more pastoral dimensions of his ministry over the past 6-7 years has been with cancer survivors, as Ric brings his experience of battling cancer to the minds and spirits of those who share in this struggle.

The trips are not as frequent now, but the ministry of Ric Masten has in good measure been a ministry on the run. And in that run a lot of lives have been touched and blessed and transformed. Ric's own awareness of his style of ministry is captured well in the following playfully self-reflective poem. While much of it sounds like it's being addressed to a particular—and unknown—individual, a broader reading of it can be seen as a message to all of those whose lives have been touched by his:

THINK OF ME AS MUSIC

Wake me in the morning
Take me to the plane
Yesterday is over now
Tomorrow never came.

It's time to get the guitar down
And hit the friendly skies
Time to have another round
Of helloes and goodbyes.

Well I guess I let my coffee
Sit there getting cold
I really didn't want it though
Just something warm to hold
While I look at you and wonder
Why a good thing has to end
And if I'll ever pass this way
And be with you again.

Gonna taxi down that runway
Turn around to go
And as we climb and circle
I'll look for you below
And somewhere in the future
Alone with my guitar
I'll sing for you
This song for you
And you know who you are.

So think of me as music
Think of me as rhyme
And if you ever need a friend
Just bring me to your mind
But like a melody,
I've just got to be
Free to drift along.
So I think I'm gonna
Change my name

And call myself a song.

In forty-seven minutes
They'll put that big bird down
I'll step into an airport
Play another town
Meet another stranger
Make another friend
Share a song...
Get it on...
And then be gone again.

So think of me as music
Think of me as rhyme
And if you ever need some love
Just bring me to your mind.
But like a melody
I've just got to be
Free to sail along.
So I think I'm gonna
Change my name
And call myself a song.

"If you ever need some love, just bring me to your mind." Such has been the nature of Ric Masten's pastoral ministry through his poetry and his appearances—leaving a little love in the hearts and minds of those whom he has touched.

CHAPTER FIVE:

The Minister/Poet—As Prophet

I guess you'd call him
a revolutionary
but he laughed real laughter
his eyes were sad
so I hung around
to hear what he had to say

he said
we have broken the ocean beyond repair
the crabs are leaving
we will soon follow

he said
we live in an insane asylum
where the sensitive go insane
that is to say go sane
but then must kill the pain
with bottle and needle

he said
the next time the conquering heroes arrive
the future is gone in a nuclear flash

he said
and there is no time left for corn
to grow

but the fact that he bothered to get out of bed
this morning and say it, gives me
a kind of hope

***Revolutionary* by Ric Masten**

Ric could not have found his way into the Unitarian Universalist family at a more tumultuous time than if he'd planned it that way. He came walking through the door just when the family inside was on the verge of tearing itself apart. His first two appearances at the denominational level were at the 1968 and 1969 General Assemblies, several years before he was granted entry into the UU ministry. Those familiar with the history of Unitarian Universalism will recognize those years as the time of the "Black Empowerment Controversy." This exceedingly painful chapter in the UU story has been well documented in other places. In very broad strokes it came down to a confrontation between those advocating integrationist versus empowerment models, and courses of action, when it came to securing racial justice; and in determining how the Association's financial resources would be used in support of one model or the other. I realize I'm using very dispassionate language now to point to an issue and to a time when passions and emotions probably ran higher that at any other period in the history of Unitarianism or Universalism.

These passions reached their peak at the 1969 General Assembly in Boston, resulting in a walk-out of a number of the delegates and the formation of a rump caucus at another locale. Prior to the walk-out the lines were clearly drawn, and the floor microphones clearly marked, as to which ones could be used in speaking to either side of the issue. There was even a move—successful for a time—to block access to the microphones designated for advocates of one of the positions.

Ric may have been the new kid on the block at the time, but that didn't stop him from speaking his piece. He was holding out for a way to get the delegates to actually talk with one another instead of just having at one another. As he recalls it: "When we got to Boston in 1969, I hated seeing what was going on. They tried to shut down the mikes. I managed to get to one and asked, 'Where's my mike? Where can we come together?' I was asking for the poetry that wasn't there." While Ric was in basic agreement with the empowerment model advocates, his attempts at some measure of reconciliation ended up placing him at odds with some of his fellow advocates—some of whom were very good friends of his. Such was the nature of the times.

Asking for, and looking for, the poetry that isn't always there—or perhaps is there but damned hard to find—goes a long way in characterizing the Ric Masten approach when it comes to the prophetic dimension of ministry. This is the dimension of ministry that seeks to advance and promote, as our UU Principles now put it, "justice, equity, and compassion in human relations… (and) the goal of world community with peace, liberty, and justice for all." The word "prophetic" in this context has nothing to do with foretelling the future in the manner that seers, astrologers, etc. purport to do. Instead it derives from the legacy of the Hebrew prophets who challenged and confronted the powers-that-be of their day as advocates for greater measures of justice and fairness for those whom Jesus would later call "the least of these." Much of Jesus' ministry, in fact, was in this Hebraic prophetic tradition; and the Unitarian Universalist principles just cited have their roots in that tradition as well.

When it comes to some of the particular issues that grow out of these broadly stated UU principles and values, especially in the latter half of the American 20th century, Ric came down on the side one would expect of a self-described "Beatie"—a cross, as already noted, between a Beat and a Hippie: Pro-Peace, Anti-War, Pro-Racial Justice, Pro-Economic Justice, Pro-Women's Rights, Pro-Gay Equality, etc. But beyond his personal stances on such issues, Ric kept much of his focus on the humanity, the often frail and fragile humanity, of those who were so diligently and passionately seeking to be on the right side of history. Rolfe Gerhart captured this aspect of Ric's ministry quite well: "He was so beautifully tuned in to the issues of women's rights and racism, and he was also so beautiful in avoiding the polarities by pointing out the polarities. He was the poetic prophet we needed so much to balance the intellectualism of our time."

Part of this dimension of Ric's ministry was also his ability to reach out, in a pastoral kind of way, to those who had become so consumed with an issue that they came close to losing sight of themselves, and whatever larger vision that had stoked their passions in the first place. His poem *The Revolutionary* is an example of this. The person who has reached the point of a destructive kind of despair is the one who needs to be reminded that he still considers it worthwhile to get up in the morning.

In holding up, by means of his poetry, his own motivations and behaviors—as well as his darker and more hidden impulses—Ric calls upon his like-minded listeners to do the same. This got him into some interesting situations and confrontations, as this story of his demonstrates:

"At the time that Black Power was an issue I had a gig at Sacramento City College. A professor in one of the congregations where I'd appeared before invited me to come to his English class at SCC. The class was about one-third Black, one-third Hispanic, and one-third White. I did a poem called *You Don't Throw Rocks, You Throw Kisses.* I'd written it for white liberals who felt black people were being rude to them or not appreciating them enough, but who still kept throwing kisses so they won't be seen as racists—or discover their own latent racism—while in the deepest part of their gut they felt like throwing rocks.

"So this young white kid got up and said to the black students, 'Aren't you offended that this white guy is taking the position of a black man in that poem?' And a black student replied, 'He's not taking the position of a black man. He is writing from his position as an observer. He's observing his behavior when he's around black people and writing about it.'"

Ric further muses: "It was the black kid who got it. He realized that I was reporting what my observer was seeing in me; and that, furthermore, my observer was talking to the young black man's observer—and observers, as such, have no race. He didn't take offence at what I was saying because it was really my observer speaking to his observer." Expanding out from this incident to his larger poetic life, Ric states, "I've taken that lesson in poetry and realized that what saved me from jumping off the bridge was my observer. Someone was watching me. The only time I don't have an observer is when the situation is too immediate—like the time I got held up in Paris and had my passport stolen. There was no observer then, I was right in the moment."

Another way to understand the observer phenomenon that Ric speaks of is to see our observer as being our capacity for self-reflection. We can look at, and scrutinize ourselves even while in the midst of what we're doing—except for those times when the situation is so immediate or so intense that our observer, or our self-reflector, gets swept aside.

Bringing it all back to the situation being described, Ric concludes, "I learned more about poetry and communication from that young black man that day than at any other time or place. He was the best teacher I ever had. As a poet I can observe myself in a racial situation and I write about it. I don't sermonize about it. I can come flat out and say I'm a racist or a sexist or whatever." It's the nakedness factor again—a willingness on Ric's part to pry open some of his deepest thoughts, feelings, and emotions in a way that will permit or cause others to do the same. The hoped for outcome is that there will be greater levels of honesty among human beings which can lead to greater levels of reconciliation.

Much of Ric's prophetic poetry, then, is a caution against self-righteousness on the part of those who so assuredly champion righteous causes. Two of his poems from the *Stark Naked* collection, which was first published in 1969 and re-issued in 1979, demonstrate this. This song/poem deals with facing the twin evils of war and the shadow side of ourselves:

PEACE PARADE

I ain't afraid of your bitter streets
And walk away from war.
I ain't afraid tho the boulevard's full of heat
And hate—an open sore.
I ain't afraid, I ain't afraid
Ain't afraid of the hate I see
But when I see all the hate in me
I'm afraid.

I ain't afraid to face the red-neck wrath
And meet their savage need.
I won't run, let 'em come an' block the path
I ain't afraid to bleed.
I ain't afraid, I ain't afraid
Ain't afraid and that's a fact.
But when I want to hit 'em back
I'm afraid.

I ain't afraid of your hard mean-eyed fuzz
With his hand carved billy-stick
Ain't afraid when the bull-horns start to buzz

> *"Peaceniks, now don't cha try no tricks!"*
> *I ain't afraid, I ain't afraid*
> *Ain't afraid of none of this*
> *But when I feel my hand become a fist*
> *I'm afraid.*
>
> *I ain't afraid to march to a public park*
> *With peace symbols over my head.*
> *And join with a few to protest the dark,*
> *Call me yella, call me red.*
> *I ain't afraid, I ain't afraid*
> *Ain't afraid of the hate in you*
> *But when I find that I can hate too*
> *I AM AFRAID.*

Then there's his poem called *The War Goes On*. In certain ways it recalls the lament of the prophet, Jeremiah, and his desperate wail of "How long, O Lord…" It's about the weariness, and the occasions of self-doubt, one experiences in trying to witness over the long haul for a peaceful dawn in the face of a seemingly endless war-making night. This is the only Masten poem of which I'm aware that is preceded by several short paragraphs of prose—and quite despairing prose at that—before poetry appears, and re-calls both the writer and the reader to a renewal of hope, however fragile that hope may be. It is a lengthy piece, and to get the necessary effect you need to take it in its entirety.

> **THE WAR GOES ON**
>
> The war goes on and once again nearly a decade later I'm called upon to sing some songs and say some things at yet another peace demonstration in another city park on another ice cream afternoon and this time I hesitate.
>
> Not because I have nothing to say about the pointless slaughter of

innocent children, but because the very ring and rhythm of that catch phrase has me in a state of déjà vu. The years of rhetoric sticking in my throat, a cracked record stuck in the same groove. Somehow I feel as though I've been here a thousand times before, talking to myself, and the war goes on.

And I hesitate, not because I think a witness against war accomplishes nothing but because I grow weary of throwing rocks at schoolboy cartoons of slobbery-teeth monsters whose names, faces, and politics change every four years. And whose legions are as frightened of me as I am of them, and yet we wear each other's spittle like a crown and the war goes on.

And I hesitate not because I grow insensitive to the suffering of others but because I begin to wonder how much the mere adventure and excitement of my being here, making this noise is not just busy work. A kind of throwing dust in the air to screen out the sight and sound of my own real loneliness and despair. In the sand of social concern behold the ostrich and the war goes on.

And I hesitate, not because I have become a war lover, fond of my eye teeth, but because I have recently discovered that I also have the seed of Eichmann in my soul, ready and waiting. To deny it, to pretend it isn't there is to give it room to grow. How can I accuse when I know that given the right climate and circumstance I am Eichmann also. I must watch myself carefully and the war goes on.

And I hesitate not because I have given up hope of seeing some new kind of dawn, but because yin comes with yang, dark with light, day with night, death with life. And if opposites help to define each other then the peace sign standing alone is only half a truth.

*And so
blinded by the pain
I am tempted to retire
from this battlefield of clarity
to meditate
and contemplate my own sad end*

*but the war goes on
and on
and on
and I find that I cannot remain
in this small gethsemane of mine
so I come to keep the vigil once again*

*this time though
the motivating impulse
is not so easy to explain
it has something to do with the fact
that a human being bothers to come in
out of a freezing killing rain*

*and so I come
and will keep coming
just as long as war goes on*

To interject a personal note, as I read these words, both the prose and the poetry, in the early weeks of the year 2007, I find I connect with much of them all too well. Even during the horror of the Vietnam War, in which I lost a high school classmate, I still felt a certain sense of hope, and even optimism, in opposing it during and immediately following my time in theological school. I did see the possibility then that people of faith and conscience could effect a turning away from violent solutions to human conflicts. And now, in the early years of my seventh decade of living, I see my country once again led into a senseless war with all its insanity and grief. This time around I feel mostly a pronounced weariness in once again attempting to confront the war makers and their folly. It is good to have Ric's reminder:

> ...that I cannot remain
> in this small gethsemane of mine
> so I come to keep the vigil once again...
>
> and so I come
> and will keep coming
> just as long as the war goes on.

Many of Ric's prophetic poems often have just the right mix of gravitas and whimsy. He can be making a quite prescient observation and statement in one second, and then having a little fun in the next—even, at times, at his own expense. In these lines from *When Giants Pass* he writes of having the shoe—his shoe—on the other foot in a racial setting, and then, well, see where it goes:

> ...
> by a route too circuitous to detail
> I come around
> in the close dusky atmosphere
> of Bethel Baptist
> abruptly aware of surroundings
> minus the glare of light off white skin
> feeling conspicuous
> unable to conform
> I bob on the surface
> of the dark moist murmuring warm
>
> what the visiting preacher

said there that evening remains a blur
yet I vividly recall the shoe
being on the other foot
and exactly
where in that packed assembly hall
that two other white faces were

afterward, at the reception
I observe the guest of honor
being shyly avoided
no one goes near him at all
he stands alone
looking tired and incredibly small
so I go up to the man and in a well-meaning
good-natured show business way
clap him on the back saying
"Working you pretty hard, are they?"

I still can't believe
I said that to Martin Luther King
and neither could he
looking up sharply
at such a blatant display of naiveté
then with patience and remarkable grace
said simply
"Yes—but it's worth it."

Moving along, Ric Masten's life and career have taken him through the pre-feminist, feminist, and post-feminist eras. Here again he displays an acute awareness of an approaching shift of the tectonic plates of gender identity, while seeing also some humor and pathos in the passing of an old order:

THE DESERTED ROOSTER

if this were a documentary
Lorne Greene would narrate
describing in his big male animal world way
the migration
as one by one the fledglings flew the coop
followed by the hen
liberated and running off to join the sisters
of a community college
singing
Gloria
Gloria
Steinem—till it becomes catholic

so far nothing new
children leaving home
a woman's victory
over the empty nest syndrome
themes done to death

but the deserted rooster is a subject
that has not yet been addressed
we know him
only as that laughable old strutter
preening and parading up and down
involved in his sexual prowess
and the sound of his own voice
up
at an ungodly hour to start the day
it was all part of the job
and there wasn't a problem
when there wasn't a choice

but picture him now
after the exodus
all alone
scratching around in his abandoned domain
looking for a good reason to get up tomorrow
and crow

if this were a documentary
it would end
focused on a stereotype weather vane
rusted on the turning point

in a changing wind.

Perhaps the most contemporary line in this poem, some three decades after it was written, is the one that says, "there wasn't a problem when there wasn't a choice." Indeed, this is the universal message that comes out of a poem written in the context of a particular time and setting. It is, in fact, the choices that the feminist movement, as it took shape in the late 1960s, made available to both women and men that have changed the nature of gender relationships since that time. In certain cases, even, the choices have been for retrenchment—to the point that in some of the more reactive circles of our society "feminist" has even become a dirty word. This is not a phenomenon to be dissected and analyzed here except to note that Ric was being more, well, prophetic than he probably even realized himself when he said "there wasn't a problem when there wasn't a choice."

Some poems, in their brevity, can speak to the consciousness of an era. The past 20 years have seen the increasing visibility, and mainstreaming, of gay and lesbian persons into American society—as well as a counter-response rooted in the deep-seated, and easily manipulated, fears that persist of homosexual human beings. This is not a topic about which Ric has written as extensively as some of his other prophetic themes, but these two short poems paint those proverbial pictures that are worth a thousand words:

MICHELANGELO

high in the scaffolding on his back
Michelangelo bites his lip—sighs
and then begins to paint the hand of God
down

below
sweeping the chapel floor
a little serf leans his broom against the wall
squints up
and with an armful of trash stumbles out
through a graceful arch
mumbling to himself

"Damn faggots."

And this one:

THE SECOND COMING

go!
tell the Catholics
tell the Protestants
the Millennium is here!
at long last
God has acknowledged
two thousand years
of prayers prayed

Jesus has reappeared
in all his glory

I know
because I saw him
at the Hospice
tenderly washing the feet
of a man who was dying
of AIDS.

Staying in the prophetic vein, Ric also addresses the post 9/11 dimension of our national life and psyche. Staying true to his blend of savvy and whimsy his poem *Outside the Box* goes from sophisticated analysis (if that's a proper way to describe poetic language) as to how and why we've become a target for terrorism, to farce in suggesting how we respond:

OUTSIDE THE BOX
America desperately needs
to spend some time
acquainting itself
with how a have-not nation must feel
constantly having to kowtow to the power we wield!
never mind billions spent on foreign aid
beneficiaries abhor their benefactors
each gift a nagging reminder of one's inadequacies
secretly the French resent and hate us
for hauling their ass out of two world wars

so forget the past
9/11 and a handful of terrorists changed all that
the stock response to such a provocative attack
is suddenly and totally passé
as the thin red line of the British will attest
we won our independence the coward's way
shooting from ambush was simply not fair play

so what do we do with the likes of Osama bin Laden?
Imprisonment?—execution?—assassination?
options that would only serve to create a martyr
his twisted convictions becoming
an even more compelling rallying point.
yet to do nothing but turn the other cheek
would work only with those of like mind

time for some thoughts
from outside the box

like
capturing bin Laden alive
our medical establishment working him over
and I mean over
removing facial hair—breast implants—
remodeling his genitals—blonding his tresses
and then in a tight-fitting cocktail dress
she's shoved out of a chopper to parachute
back into the heart of Afghanistan

the Taliban terrorist may be willing to commit suicide
for his fundamentalist belief
but face punishment with this diabolically clever?
and risk becoming a woman?
Never!

In this book's opening chapter I noted that one of the roles Ric Masten assumes in addressing admittedly "serious" issues is that of the court jester. The court jester knew what was going on, and while his role was to make the monarch laugh he was also looking to plant a seed of insight or revelation in the monarch's mind. I would call the above a court jester poem. The farcical notion of sending a re-genderized bin Laden back to Afghanistan is good for a laugh; but it is offered in a poem that also calls on its readers and hearers to try to understand how the supposed "benevolence" of the world's most powerful nation can create a resentment and an anger we can barely comprehend—until it quite literally blows up in our faces. And even then we don't usually get it, unless maybe a poet can turn on the light for us.

In his Foreword to a collection of Ric's poems titled *I Know It Isn't Funny But...* Jim Parkman makes a similar point. He writes, "Good humored people who smile as they talk are sneaky. We tend not to think of them as revolutionaries and radicals when they are. Ric Masten is one example. What he says is penetrating and, sometimes, painful...And he does it by smiling through his writing."

Smiling through his writing and looking for the poetry when it is least apparent describes in large measure how Ric Masten has carried out the prophetic piece of his poetic, troubadour ministry. He asked, "Where's my mike?"—i.e. "How can I offer you my voice?"—in seeking some human reconciliation while good and decent people were tearing themselves apart over an extremely painful issue. He playfully heralded the second coming of Christ while pointing to an act of compassion for an AIDS victim. And he calls on his readers—sometimes playfully and sometimes not—to examine their own motives, and even their shadow sides, as they so devotedly strive to do the right thing. These are the kinds of things a good minister, and a good prophet, does.

CHAPTER SIX:

The Minister/Poet—As Theologian

when
the shadow of death
fell upon us
the queen mother died
and the swarm
scattered
far afield
social insects
self-aware now
feeling utterly alone

except

in our dreams
songs
and poetry

there
through it all
the voice of the hive

calling us home

The Voice of the Hive by Ric Masten

what we hear in the music hall
see in the galleries
what the poets say
and dancers do

ah

this is religion

From...*The Priests Most High* by Ric Masten

John Buehrens recalls this Ric Masten story from seminary days in the early 1970s: "I was the leader of the UU students in the Boston area while going to Harvard Divinity School and I got Ric to come do a performance for us. We were in the Brown Room at HDS and who shows up to hear Ric do his thing but Joe Bassett. Joe, who is a life-long UU out of Northboro, Massachusetts, occupies the theological right of Unitarian Universalism. He's always been deeply interested in the theological positions of his fellow UUs and concerned about the sloppiness of their theology, and likes to press them on what their theological positions really are. He also has a sense, a la Karl Barth, that the church exists in part to criticize the State, so he's always had a grudging respect for people whose prophetic stance is less than adequately (in his view) theologically grounded.

"So he shows up to hear Ric. When it came time for some Q & A he asked Ric if he identified with the Stephen Fritchman school of West Coast Humanism, or did he categorize himself as being more influenced by existentialism—Tillichian existentialism in particular (which Joe himself did not care for)."

As John tells it, "Ric just sat there in silence for a few seconds, and then replied 'Huh?'"

Buehrens adds: "The other theological students were similarly nonplussed. This was an era when most of us were not willing to categorize ourselves theologically, and more of us identified with Ric's 'Huh?' than with Joe's question."

Rev. Bassett's concerns about sloppy theology notwithstanding (and not without their legitimacy either), Ric's ministry—and his own brand and style of theology—were actually anticipated some three to four decades before he came onto the scene by one of the premier Unitarian ministers of the 20th century, the Rev. John Haynes Holmes. In an essay published in the 1935 edition of *The Beacon Song and Service Book* Holmes wrote: "When I say 'God' it is poetry and not theology. Nothing that any theologian has ever written about God has helped me much, but everything that poets have written about flowers, and birds, and skies, and seas, and God—whoever He [sic] may be—has at one time or another reached my soul!...The theologians gather dust upon the shelves of my library, but the poets are stained with my fingers and blotted with my tears. I never seem so near the truth as when I care not what I think or believe, but only (when I am) with these masters of inner vision."

Holmes was the minister of the Community Church of New York for 42 years (1907-1949). He was among the founders of the NAACP, the American Civil Liberties Union, and the Fellowship of Reconciliation. As controversial as his resolute pacifism became with his fellow Unitarians—clergy and laity alike—during two World Wars, his professional stature and integrity were unparalleled and unquestioned. I find it remarkable that this most remarkable member of America's liberal clergy during the 20th century would so straightforwardly declare his affinity for the poet over the theologian. One can only speculate on what a meeting of the Rev. Holmes and the Rev. Masten would have been like. Would Ric's poetic, troubadour style of ministry, and theology, have brought Holmes "so near the truth" for which he strove?

The question of whether or not Masten's poetic magic would have worked for John Haynes Holmes will never be answered, but it has certainly worked for plenty of others both within and well beyond

Unitarian Universalist circles. And Holmes' dichotomy notwithstanding, the poet, the artist, and the theologian, each in their own way, perform the same task. They each and all call us to an awareness of a reality greater than ourselves—however that reality may be named. They seek to lift us beyond the bounds of the oft-confining, and sometimes imprisoning, self and put us in touch with parts of ourselves and our wider world and universe we scarcely knew existed. The theologian may go about this task in a more academic fashion by both challenging and stretching our minds when it comes to our pursuit of the Ultimate; the poet and the artist aim more for our hearts, souls, and emotions. Consider this Ric Masten story, told by an academic—a Professor of History in this case—about his resistance, and then capitulation, to the Masten magic in a secular setting in Monterey, California:

"The first time I saw Ric Masten I was prepared not to like him. We appeared on the same bill the evening the Monterey Bay Aquarium celebrated its 15th anniversary. There were over a thousand people in the auditorium and the agenda was very tight. If you go over ten minutes, they warned, we will drag you from the stage. I jammed through my presentation and sat back down in the front row, hoping the program would be over so I could go out and get a beer.

"Then they announced Ric Masten. He strolled out to the center of the stage with an acoustic guitar and there was a nice surge of applause. What's this? Oh, Jesus, I thought. A hippie. I thought all the hippies were either dead or had metamorphosed into stockbrokers. They kept the agenda tight for this? He did a couple of songs that I can't even remember now, but I do remember clenching my fists and refusing to clap along with him. Clap along. Right. Clap this. Then he announced his last song, and through the haze of cynicism and impatience I heard a simple refrain: 'Let It Be a Dance.' By the second verse I was leaning to hear the words and by the last chorus I was standing with the rest of them, singing along, tears streaming down my cheeks, smiling like an idiot. With one transparent, sweet, lovely song he had turned me into a blubbering fool. Who was this Pied Piper of a man who could uplift us all with such a simple song while fighting a disease that was killing him as he sang?"

Yes, it's a good and moving story. The teller is Sandy Lydon, Historian Emeritus at Cabrillo College in Aptos, California. But is there any way Ric is playing the role of a theologian in this instance? Yes, I would say, in this manner: He took an individual from a sense of isolation, and by his own acknowledgement "cynicism and impatience," to catching him, completely unaware, with the metaphor of a dance. Ric took Sandy from his own alone-ness to a sense of connection with something greater than himself, which got him—completely against his own instincts—up on his feet and clapping and singing with a room full of a thousand other souls.

Theology, literally translated, means "knowledge of God." But such knowledge need not, and should not, be limited to intellectual constructs about the existence or non-existence of a Supreme Being. It can also mean knowledge as an awareness of one's relationship with and participation in—a "dance" if you will—all of Life Itself. The term "logos," as it is contained in the word "theology" does not just mean intellectual knowledge, valuable and necessary as such knowledge is. It refers as well to the ways in which we "know" with all of our senses. This, in fact, is what the poet and the artist do; they call us to greater levels of knowing with all of our senses. To make one more pass at John Haynes Holmes, in an essay titled *What God Means to Me* he wrote: "God is the Life-Spirit of the world, working unconsciously in nature and consciously in man [sic]..." Indeed, it is poetry that connects us to this Life-Spirit of the world and universe. No wonder Holmes preferred the poets to the theologians!

One of the crucial tasks of ministry, then, is to be a theologian in the sense just indicated. The minister-as-theologian is the one who calls, guides, and directs those with whom he or she ministers to an awareness of their connection to and with the Life-Spirit. At the time when Ric Masten was granted entry to the Unitarian Universalist ministry this kind of calling and guiding, by most of the rank and file UU clergy, was done largely on an intellectual level. I do not disparage intellectualism, as I've long enjoyed the life of the mind. But the challenge Ric brought to his fellow members in the UU clergy during the late 1960s, and on through the 70s, was an alternative way of fulfilling the minister/theologian role. He did not challenge the strong intellectual bent of the UU ministers of that era in any direct way. He just did theology in a different way.

Consider the poem *The Voice of the Hive*, as shown at the beginning of this chapter. If a UU minister of the era just cited were to offer a sermon on the same subject as this poem he—and at least nine times out of ten it would have been a "he"—would have held forth on the topic of existential alone-ness and anxiety with the appropriate doses of Heidegger, Sartre, and Tillich mixed in. Then he would have moved into an exploration of the possibilities, although we can't say for sure, of maybe locating the locus of one's Ground of Being in an indifferent Universe. Such a sermon may well have been a well-crafted, carefully thought out, and articulately delivered address (not, ahem, unlike some of those I pulled off in the early days of my ministry!). But it may well have left a good number of those in his congregation with the same response that Ric had after hearing Rev. Bassett's question: "Huh?"

Now, look at the image of a swarm of bees forced out of their hive: "…scattered far afield…self-aware now…feeling utterly alone…" while looking for the "voice of the hive…calling us home." Here is a way to grasp or imagine the need both for human community and a sense of cosmic connection in a world that can often feel like an alien land. In such a place we are called and challenged to listen for the "voices" that call us to be at home in our world and universe. Practically anyone hearing or reading this poem knows what that feeling of alone-ness is like, especially when some of the props we live by get kicked loose—"when the queen bee dies" that is to say. We may not know the origin or the name of the voice that calls us home, but we yearn for it and listen for it nonetheless. We strive towards that which endures in the midst of the transience of our lives, whether we call it "God," or something else, or by no name at all. This, as I see it, is the "sermon" contained in these few lines of poetry.

Even as Rev. Buehrens enjoys telling the "Huh?" story, he also understands and deeply appreciates the religious nature of Ric's work and ministry:

"What makes Ric's work religious, obviously, is not overt pietism or religious language. But religion is not really in those things. It's not even in belief or doubt. In all cultures and in all lives religion is to be found in our human response to the dual reality of being alive and having to die. What makes Ric's work religious is his capacity to frame words that help us see our mortal lives afresh—in all their fallibility, fragility, and funniness. To be more honest. More open. More grateful for one another and for the gift of life. And then to rise refreshed to try to live our finite lives with greater caring.

"Ministers themselves do not endure eternally, God knows. But they do help to reveal, hidden in the midst of the transience of life, what does endure. Through insights often more than one-liners, they help us see the enduring. And to live closer to it. Because of that Ric's ministry does and will endure."

The reference to religion as "our human response to the dual reality of being alive and having to die" is a definition put forth by one of our colleagues in the UU ministry, Rev. Forrest Church. To phrase it in a slightly different way, religion is how we say "yes" to Life in the face of the reality and inevitability of death. Theology is the language we use, inadequate as it will always be, in giving voice to that "yes." The story of how Ric came to write his signature song and work, *Let It Be a Dance* (the song that turned Sandy Lydon into a "blubbering fool") is really a working out of this understanding of religion and theology. Here's Ric telling it in his own words:

"It was one of those horrendous tragedies that happen in the American high schools every 4 or 5 years. This particular incident took place one December at Carmel High School. A first year teacher, Sharon Elliot, offered a course on modern dance, and had 14 young women and men performing like Broadway professionals. My two oldest daughters, Jerri and April, took the class and were a regular part of the troupe. During Christmas vacation Sharon saw that a famous ensemble out of New York City was performing in San Jose, about 80 miles from Carmel. She called up all her students and said that if they were willing to be crowded during the journey they could go up to San Jose in her VW bus. Both of my daughters wanted to go in the worst way but had other holiday engagements scheduled.

"As the carload of dancers was rounding a corner on the way home a drunk driver who had pulled over to the side of the road decided to pull back onto the highway without looking behind him. The VW bus crashed headlong into his car, killing the two front seat passengers, one of whom was the teacher, and a back seat passenger. All the other girls and boys in the back seats were seriously injured.

"One of those injured was Barbara Brussell, my daughter Jerri's best friend at the time. Her sister Bonnie was one of the passengers who got killed. Barbara's kneecap was so badly damaged that the doctor doubted if she would ever walk again without a cane, let alone dance again. My family and I visited Barbara in the hospital where I made a bet with her. I wagered that she would come dancing up our Big Sur dirt road exactly one year from that day. And what's more, I would write the music that she would be dancing to.

"The following week, while working in my garden, the entire song arrived. I ran to the house and wrote the lyrics down as fast as I could type. Better still, the words came along with a melody. Barbara Brussell, now a well known cabaret singer in New York City, did come dancing up our country road exactly a year to the day after the accident, with me singing and playing *Let It Be A Dance*. Barbara was limping, it's true—but DANCING!"

The image, and the reality, of the dance has become the anchoring metaphor for Ric's ministry. It is an affirmation of the enduring power of the Life Spirit, even in the face of death. Unitarian Universalists do not have an established creed, and do not read from a prayer book in their worship; and yet this affirmation of faith is repeated whenever Unitarian Universalists turn to Hymn #311 in their hymnal and sing this song:

LET IT BE A DANCE

Let it be a dance we do
May I have this dance with you
Through the good times
And the bad times too
Let it be a dance.

Let a dancing song be heard
Play the music, say the words
And fill the sky with sailing birds
And let it be a dance.

Learn to follow, learn to lead
Feel the rhythm, fill the need
To reap the harvest plant the seed
And let it be a dance.

Everybody turn and spin
Let your body learn to bend
And like a willow in the wind
Let it be a dance.

A child is born the old must die
A time for joy a time to cry
So take it as it passes by
And let it be a dance.

The morning star comes out at night
Without the darkness there's no light
If nothing's wrong then nothing's right
So let it be a dance.

Let the sun shine, let it rain
Share the laughter, bare the pain
And round and round we go again
So let it be a dance.

A play on just a single word and phrase in that final verse has both a pastoral and a theological life all its own. The phrase is "bear the pain." Ric can tell the story:

"When I wrote and typed the song in the first place I meant the word to be 'bear' the pain. Then I was doing a program in a mental institution early on in the history of the song. There was a woman sitting before me on the floor who seemed to be really in to what I was doing. She laughed the loudest and openly wept in all the right places. But when I sang *Let It Be a Dance* to end my program she darkened visibly. As it turned out she was the director of the place (these days you can't tell the players from the fans). She told me I'd wrecked my whole program with my last song. Feeling on the defensive I told her I thought I'd underlined it with my final song/poem. As we talked on I saw she was disturbed by the phrase "bear the pain" when it should be "bare the pain."

Taking it from there, Ric goes on: "Yes, 'bare' not 'bear.' That makes all the difference! This institution, in fact a good part of the speaking world, is inhabited by people who don't know how to spell the word correctly. We must learn not to bear the pain—not to keep it bottled up inside. Rather we should bare it—share it, unburden ourselves of the sorrow and pain that come with life. Since then it has always been 'bare.'"

Then, there's this final twist: "I have a perverse nature. When the

UU Hymnal Committee asked me if they could use the song, they asked if I'd mind if they changed the melody a bit for the new hymnal. I didn't care. But out of orneriness and playfulness I decided to send the Committee a page clipped from one on my published books with the lyrics printed without my bear/bare commentary. I wanted to see what they would do. Well they changed the spelling back from 'bare' to 'bear' which tickled me greatly. When they sent me a copy of the manuscript to proof-read I kept mum about what they'd done. Why? Because that typo has given me the punch line for every concert and reading I've done since then. I even use the bear/bare spelling difference when I officiate weddings—counseling the couple about how the word must be spelled to have a successful marriage."

Indeed, Ric did do the bear/bare comparison when he appeared at my church in October of 2005. I can tell exactly which hymnals were used on that day by turning to Number 311 and seeing which ones have the word "bear" crossed out and replaced with "bare!"

The message is clear enough, and needs no belaboring. The pastoral and theological challenge and question it raises is how much of ourselves do we "bare" to ourselves, to those we care about and trust the most, and to whatever we sense and believe to be greater than ourselves.

Religion is our human response to the dual reality of being alive and knowing we will die. Religion is how we say Yes to Life in the face of death. Theology is how we give voice to this truth. The story of how this song came to be written, and the words that Ric took from his garden to his typewriter, are a playing out of these definitions. Many years later, as some closing words to a collection of his work, Ric wrote a Coda to his signature song:

DANCE BENEDICTION

Yes!
let it be a dance
let life be a dance

THE MINISTER/POET—AS THEOLOGIAN　　　　　　　　　　　　　　**81**

because we dance to dance
not to go anywhere

and let it be a dance
let life be a dance
because within the dance
we move easily with the paradox
knowing
that for every step forward
there must be a step back

and anything else
would have us marching
away from the music.

Ric is a sneaky theologian in the sense that the theology in his poems sneaks up on you. You're not aware you're reading theology, and Ric may not even be aware he's writing it! In fact, he may even disavow the title "theologian" altogether. But the theology is there in his poetry for those with ears to hear and minds to understand and souls to be uplifted. And even a poet/theologian like Ric (acknowledged or not) can resort to a little prose now and then in describing his life-stance—as he does in these musings:

"I call myself a 'non-theist'. I've come a long, long way from my upbringing which was 'atheist.' I've softened a great deal since my smart-assed, hair-brained youth. I'm far from being against whatever folks use to see them through the night; that is, unless, they come after me with their 'absolute truth.'"

"In the forest of religion we all look for the tree that we feel most comfortable sitting under. The problem is that once we find that special tree, we want to start clear cutting back every other tree in the forest. I describe the Unitarian Universalist belief not as a tree but as a clearing in the forest of all things where one can go and work out one's salvation with or without the help of like-minded others. I have yet to meet a Unitarian Universalist with whom I agreed totally, or who totally agreed with me. And that is the beauty of it."

On the subject of free will and free choice, the Rev. Masten's take on the subject is very close to that of one of the 20th century's premier theologians, Paul Tillich, who maintained that we are creatures of "finite freedom." While not using Tillichian language, here's how Ric puts it:

"I don't believe in personal 'free choice.' I've never made a choice that wasn't based on a multitude of things I didn't choose —IQ, inherited DNA, the beliefs and non-beliefs of the family I happened to be born into and raised by—and the teachers to whom I was assigned, the accidents that befell me, the sicknesses I've had, a million chance encounters, books I was given to read, etc. I could go on forever, but all of the above and more is what I base my so called personal free choice on. In the end, however, I do believe in free choice—joint free choice. You and I together choosing. Two people exchanging ideas are adding to each other, and at any given moment in this 'give and take' the possibility of making different personal choices is always present."

On the subject of the religious body that granted him ministerial status, Ric offers this:

"In 1971 I put in for Fellowship as a Unitarian Universalist minister. I had no college degree and refused to go to seminary. But I told them I was a minister-at-large and that I'd been traveling the country for four years at that point at their expense doing what I do. They hemmed and hawed but finally took me aboard as a Unitarian Universalist Troubadour Minister. I am one of a kind. I am the only Unitarian minister in history with no college degree or seminary education."

Ric Masten's subtle and poetic way of being a theologian continues to reach those within the communion of Unitarian Universalism and far beyond it as well. Recall Professor Lydon's question: "Who was this Pied Piper of a man who could uplift us all with such a simple song while fighting a disease that was killing him as he sang?" The reference here is to the battle with prostate cancer Ric's been dealing with since 1999, a battle that has taken that previously cited definition of religion out of the abstract and given it an all-too-real reality for Ric. His life and ministry for the past seven years of up and down PSA numbers has indeed been his human response to the dual reality of being alive and knowing one will die. But then Ric has made a career out of making religion and theology real. As will be seen in a later chapter, he calls the past seven years "the ministry for which I've been preparing all my life."

CHAPTER SEVEN:

The Minister/Poet—As Colleague

not long ago these grand
gray-maned gargantuans
ruled the theological plain
Oratorus Rex!
the rest of us jumping up and down
like toy poodles
at the neck of Great Danes
but in the muck discourse
that followed dinner last night
the dinosaur
came to the end of his reign

there
mired in a tar pit
of yesterday's thinking
unable to free themselves
from too much Chardonnay
they bellowed and raged—thrashing about
sawing the charged air with their teeth
bewildered—wounded—feeling betrayed
no longer influential enough
to throw their weight around
they went down slowly
glaring directly into our eyes

today their reputation
is all that remains
left like petrified footprints
to be measured and intellectualized by smaller
more maneuverable creatures
unable to fully comprehend
the enormous size and majesty
these giants once had

there is always something about

a change for the better
that is terribly
sad

Oratorus Rex! by Ric Masten

The reason clichés become clichés is because they contain just enough truth to allow them to be credibly repeated over and over. One such cliché is that the ministry is a lonely profession and calling even as it demands that the minister be a public person. Ministers can be on friendly terms, and even socialize, with members of their congregations. Ministers are also granted entry into some of the most intensely personal places in the lives their congregants. But when it comes to those places where, and persons with whom, ministers can be open, relaxed, and free in confiding about the more personal places of their lives the pickings are pretty slim. They can develop circles of friends and confidants completely apart from their ministerial life; and/or they can turn to their ministerial colleagues who know what it's like to be there.

Ric Masten—the Rev. Ric Masten—has done both. He has a wider constituency well beyond the UU community where he does not wear, and has no need to wear, his minister's hat. At the same time he has cultivated relationships with his ministerial colleagues over the years that have proven to be deeply rewarding both to Ric and to the ministers who have been a part of his life. By the time he formally entered the Unitarian Universalist ministry he had already developed a network of friends and contacts among the UU clergy of that time. It was generally the settled UU ministers, along with the UUA field staff, who served as his de-facto booking agents when he was on the Billings Lecture circuit. After the Billings money ran out, Ric continued to turn to these ministers—while also expanding his contacts among his new-found colleagues—to keep his troubadour ministry alive and well and ever-growing.

So, after growing up with virtually no contact or dealings with any kind of religious community, and only five years down the road from the first time he and Billie walked into a UU church, Ric found himself to be a UU minister. A lot of the folks who'd been getting him gigs were now his colleagues. This made for a shift in relationship. Due largely to his unique position with his fellow UU clergy as a circuit riding, troubadour minister, Ric was in unknown territory, and on a steep learning curve about what this new relationship meant. Being in town one day and on the road the next often put him in the position of hearing the confessions of his newfound colleagues, even though this was not a role he'd asked for. Ric recalls, "I'd come into these ministers' homes and they would quickly confide in me. The minister would tell me about the 'woman' in the congregation, or about how he and his wife were getting a divorce, or about how he was getting beat up by his church. I'd hear all this in these guys' houses."

His slip-ups came when he conveyed such information to other clergy whom he would later visit. "I shot off my mouth a few times when I shouldn't have," Ric acknowledges. His intention was really to alert a minister, or ministers, as to how some of their colleagues were hurting—which is fine, provided it's been cleared with the hurting minister in the first place. That was the piece Ric missed a couple of times. But, as noted, it was all part of the process of learning what it meant to be a colleague while on the road and on the run.

Whatever those initial mis-steps may have been, out of Ric's contacts over the years have come some very close and enduring relationships and a treasure trove of stories. Given the fact that, by his own estimate, Ric has appeared in some 500 UU congregations over the past 40 years, and has probably come into contact with several hundred UU clergypersons during that time, the stories that have accumulated would be beyond the scope of even a single book, much less a single chapter in a book. The hope is that the stories told here will at least give a flavor of the kind of ministry Ric carried forth with his ministerial colleagues.

He started close to home. After his discovery by Rosemary and Howard Matson, and his West Coast/Central Pacific UU debut at Asilomar, Ric began getting gigs at nearby UU churches. An early one was at the UU church in San Jose where the minister was Rev. Byrd Hillegas. By his own telling, Ric met resistance in getting invites to pulpits where the ministers were well known speakers and orators. But Byrd extended an invite. When I asked him, as Ric recalls, why he was taking a chance on me, Byrd answered, "I figure I can't lose. If you come and you're horrible and my congregation wants to know what I was doing in inviting you I'll just say I heard you were good, but it won't happen again. And if you're a shinning star, then I'm the one they're going to thank!"

This was at the time that Ric was doing his bead ministry which he brought to his San Jose appearance, and said a little about how and why he was doing it. Ric picks up the story: " It (the San Jose church) was full. So I do my thing and I'm taking my bows, and then I saw Byrd stand up. He came up and spread out his arms and yells, 'It happened, it happened here today…' and he reached in his pocket and pulled out a string of beads and put them around my neck and gave me a big hug while the whole congregation stood and clapped.

And while they were clapping and cheering Byrd whispered in my ear, 'That'll teach you, you little son of a bitch!'"

But it was also from Byrd that Ric learned the meaning of true collegiality: "At the second Asilomar conference I was really down. While walking up a trail I saw Byrd coming. He saw me and saw my demeanor and said, 'I'll be whatever you need me to be—a brother, a friend, a father, a minister.' Somehow he sensed something was amiss and he became whatever I needed at that time."

The relationships among the UU clergy of that time—the 1960s and 70s—took place within the confines of an almost entirely male dominated domain. "Fraternity" is not an inaccurate term for it. There was a kind of hale-fellow camaraderie, and an even genuine caring for one another. But just below the surface a subtle—and not always so subtle—kind of one-ups-manship was also going on:

"Then there was a time with Glenn Turner and his church up in Tacoma. I put these beads on Glenn and he immediately took off his flowered tie and put it on me. Byrd had come to live up there by then to be with his son. So I look up and see this bald guy coming forward. It was Byrd. He gets up there, says a few words, and then puts this bowling trophy on a rope around my neck; and I looked at it and it said Second Place."

Glenn could be both jovial and confrontational with Ric all at the same time and about the same issue. This is, in fact, one of the marks of a healthy collegial relationship. It needs humor—even when the humor has an edge—but it can also evoke loving challenges in certain situations. We've already seen some of Glenn and Ric's dealings with one another over *The Bixby Bridge Incident* poem in Chapter Three as they exchanged letters about the appropriateness of Ric's reading that poem while out on the UU church circuit. As Glenn recalls, he first heard about the poem from Ric himself: "He (Ric) called me in Tacoma and said he'd just come back from a bridge and was feeling so depressed that he'd thought about jumping, thinking that his life was half-empty. But then he said he realized that if his life was half-empty it was also half full, so he stepped back and wrote a poem about it. And I said to him, right there over the phone, 'Dammit it Ric, you'll do anything for material!'"

But Glenn shifted from this collegial kind of jostling and jousting to coming straight at Ric when he felt Ric crossed a line. But even with his challenges, Glenn was truly worried about Ric's state of mind. Returning to Rev. Turner's previously cited letter: "Ric, I don't envy your situation. I think a road show surrounds a person with intolerable pressures. You appear now as driven, harried, and anxious. I've caught a glimmer of a different Ric Masten and I cherish what could be there. You have a friend here who cares a good deal about you. I really hate to see the pain." As we also saw in Chapter Three, it was Ric's response to Glenn's reaching out to him that probably saved his ministry when this matter got to the Ministerial Fellowship Committee.

Ric and Glenn's relationship was actually strengthened by this confrontation, and yielded other fond memories in the years that followed. Here's one more from a later stage in Glenn's ministry: "Years later when I was in Sherborne, Massachusetts Ric came to see us and my [then] father-in-law was there. He was a very conservative guy. He saw Ric in what looked to him like some kind of hippie affectation, including a leather binder he was carrying, and said 'Well, I see you have your saddle bags; where's your horse?' Ric came right back at him and the two of them went at it like a couple of cats. But by the time Ric left the house they were fast buddies. That's how Ric was. He could meet people where they were, and go hell for leather with them, and then come out friends."

The bag in question here was one that had been made for Ric to help him organize and carry his poems and music. Ric remembers it fondly: "A hippie kid wanted to give me a present so he made me this leather binder to carry my music and poems in. It also had a place for my music stand. It was a beautiful leather saddle bag kind of deal. So I carried this thing that looked like a saddle bag into Glenn's house—and that was what set things off between his father-in-law and me."

It was this ability of Ric's to connect with people who may not have been in the same place as he was on this or that particular issue that points to one of the ironies of his collegial relationships with his fellow UU clergy. However much he may have been seen, rightly or not, as a Beat/Hippie/Radical/Poet/Songster, he received some of his more welcoming and accepting overtures from those ministers who were seen, again rightly or not, as being in the more traditional wing of the UU movement. As Ric himself observed, "The more traditional or conservative guys tended to invite me to their churches and pulpits more than the liberal or radical guys. I don't know why but they did."

The first invitation Ric received, in fact, for a church appearance after being granted Preliminary Fellowship into the UU ministry came from Rev. Carl Scovel, the long time, and now retired, minister of Boston's King's Chapel. Of the more than 1000 congregations in the UUA, King's Chapel has the most definitively liberal Christian theology and the most formal and liturgically structured worship services. Carl was the one, as noted earlier, who came out from the Fellowship Committee's meeting room at the Starr King School to inform Ric that he had passed muster with them. In the same conversation Carl invited Ric to come to King's Chapel. Ric accepted.

He was still in work-shirt, levis, and bead mode then, but seeing as it was King's Chapel Ric did wear a sport coat, minus the tie. Rev. Scovel told Ric it was his moment to do as he wanted, and he did his usual gig. It was the after-effects of the service that produced the most lasting memories for Ric:

"Afterwards I'm standing at the door and these little old ladies are coming out. The first one says to me, 'Well, I knew we were in for something this morning when you climbed into the pulpit and didn't have a tie on. That's how I knew we were in real trouble for today!' Another one came by and told me about the busts of all the former King's Chapel ministers that are displayed in its chapel. 'Go back down the right side of King's Chapel and you'll see the busts,' she said, 'My great-great grandfather is the sixth one down the row there. You will see that he has very wavy hair; and this morning, Mr. Masten, it was standing straight on end!' The last one was this very tiny woman who said to me, 'Mr. Masten, my name is Mrs. Statler of the Statler/Hilton Hotels.' I thought maybe she was going to offer me some kind of lucrative deal, or give me access to the Hilton hotels, but instead she added, 'And I want to tell you this morning that I hate Mr. Hilton!' Carl was standing next to me, and I gave him this rather puzzled look. He just smiled and shrugged and said, 'Every Sunday.'"

One of Ric's more poignant memories of a collegial moment involves the Rev. Max Gaebler in Madison, Wisconsin. Max and Ric were on different sides of the aforementioned Black Empowerment Controversy, which didn't stop Max from inviting Ric to Madison when he was on the Billings circuit. Here's what happened that evening: "It was snowing and my appearance was at the college [University of Wisconsin], and I did the Bixby poem. We drove back to Max's house through the snow in silence, with just the tires crunching in the snow. We pulled into the driveway and Max just sat there, not getting out of the car. I wondered what was going to happen and then he asked me if I'd ever read *The Bell Jar* by Sylvia Plath. I told him I had. It was the setting in the snow and the quiet car that gave the event its impact. With the snow coming down and Max hanging onto the steering wheel he told me he was the basis for the minister Ms. Plath made fun of in her novel. And then he asked, 'What could I have said that might have made a difference?'"

It was the simple humanity and the simple deeds of kindness that his fellow UU clergy extended to him that meant much more to Ric than their theology, or their political positions, or their institutional standing and institutional aspirations. For example: "I remember Paul Carnes in Buffalo, New York. More than once he drove over a hundred miles to pick me up somewhere so I could come to his church. Later he ran against Jack Mendelsohn for UUA President. I was probably more in line with Mendelsohn's positions, but I supported Paul. In all the times that I came through Chicago Jack never invited me to come to his church [First Unitarian—Chicago]. My dearest friends, Howard and Rosemary Matson, were Mendelsohn supporters in his bid for the UUA Presidency, and they were pretty upset with me for backing Carnes." Here's how Ric closed the deal: "I told Rosemary that three times Paul had driven great distances to have me in his church while Mendelsohn had turned down my request to appear in his church. 'Who would you vote for?' I asked her."

Paul Carnes was elected, but his term was cut short when he died of cancer in January of 1979. Paul and Ric did have a final, and deeply felt encounter: "There's a sweet ending here that I may be living myself. Twenty-four days before Paul died he came to a District meeting up in the Seattle area where I was also on the program. When I think about how tired I get from chemotherapy I can't imagine how Paul did it. Luckily I was put at his table and I was able to thank him for how wonderful he'd been with me, particularly when I was having marital problems and he'd told me about some of his own. He'd gotten through it just as Billie and I did. So I got to thank him twenty-four days before he died."

There is a playful side to Ric Masten that often had a way of bringing out a certain kind of playfulness on the part of his colleagues. Rolfe Gerhart, now living in retirement in Maine, recalls a story from his earlier Maine days when he was Ric's Billings Lecture contact for the Northeast District:

"I was in my late 20s and his poetry was speaking to me right where I was. I loved setting things up for him. Ric was sophisticated and naïve at the same time. If you were to pick an archetype he'd be the holy innocent. He had a natural innocent quality about him. I remember I was taking him to Holton, Maine and then over to St. Johns in New Brunswick. He must have flown in to Bangor. We got to the border crossing and we were wondering how the border guards would take this guitar toting hippie who seemed a little too old for most of the hippies they'd seen. Well, we got through that fine; no searches or anything. Then we got over into Canada about 10 miles

THE MINISTER/POET—AS COLLEAGUE **93**

and I decided to take advantage of Ric's naiveté and said, 'Ric, look! There's a Canadian crow!' And Ric said, 'Oh wow, a Canadian crow!' We drove along a little further and Ric said, 'Uh Rolfe, what's the difference about a Canadian crow?' I said, 'Ric, a Canadian crow is a crow in Canada!' He took jokes well."

In his retirement—after settlements in San Antonio, Texas, Richmond, Virginia, and Rockland, Maine—Rolfe now lives in Thomaston, Maine where he makes and sells mandolins. He showed my wife and me a picture of a guitar he'd made for Ric, which they had designed in 1972 when Rolfe was in San Antonio and Ric performed there: "This was the first guitar I built from scratch with Brazilian rosewood, which you can hardly get today. At that time I probably paid around $30.00 or $40.00 for it. The same wood would cost around five grand now. We carefully measured the Yamaha he had then as he liked the size of the neck. And I put some unique bracing on the top because he traveled a lot and liked to fly with it strung up to full tension, and so needed extra strength. I did some inlays on some of the frets. There's a yin/yang on this one, and a homesick snail on the 7th fret and a sunflower above the snail. The 12th fret is the octave where you start over, so I have the Bixby Bridge, which is where Ric started over. Those inlays were special to him." Ric still has the guitar, and while he uses it sparingly these days—mostly at the weddings he officiates—he regards is as being among his most prized possessions.

Numerous stories remain out there from those days of the sixties and seventies, and Mwalimu Imara's aforementioned characterization of Ric as a troubadour of "love and sanity during insane times" is certainly an apt one. A few other short-takes from that era include the following:

Rev. Bob Eddy, Minister Emeritus of the UU Church in Pensacola, Florida: "I have warm memories of Ric's concerts and the GA when he asked for a mike in the middle during the fractious BAC verses BAWA debate. [BAC stood for Black Affairs Council and represented the empowerment advocates. BAWA stood for Black and White Action and represented the integrationist advocates.] I remember his skill in warming up so many different kinds of audiences. He was a true troubadour. And I also remember that he wouldn't eat breakfast on the road because it was the only meal he could refuse graciously."

Rev. Gordon Gibson, now retired from the Elkhart, Indiana UU congregation: "My main memory was of Ric and his daughter coming to Jackson, Mississippi in 1970 or 71. He said he liked to work and I took him at his word. He was in town for a day and a half and I had him do a poetry workshop at Jackson State University (a primarily African-American university), a coffee house gig at Milsaps College, and may have worked in one or two other things. I just about wore the poor boy out. Here in Elkhart, Indiana he is remembered for several visits, both with my predecessor, Bob Dick, and with me. Those who remember him love him."

Rev. Ken Brown, District Executive for the Pacific Central District, has come to know Ric in more recent times: "What I can say about Ric from my personal relationship is the importance of family to him. We, my wife and I, have spent time at his and Billie's house with daughters and husbands and grandchildren. We've even gone to his grandson's Little League games as it was one way we could get together when we were in town."

A very heartfelt, and multi-layered, tribute to Ric comes from Rev. Tom Owen-Towle as he and his wife (and co-minister) Carolyn Owen-Towle, have long and often crossed paths with Ric and Billie. When Ric's mother sent her son to study art at Pomona College, he studied under Professor Millard Sheets. While Ric flunked out of Pomona he was able to demonstrate to Mr. Sheets a fine artistic ability. Here's where Tom picks up the story:

"One of our family's prized moments was when Billie Barbara and Ric actually went on a pilgrimage to connect with Ric's early art master, Millard Sheets at his family compound in Gualala, California, overlooking the Pacific Ocean. Ric asked Millard what made him tick

THE MINISTER/POET—AS COLLEAGUE

as a genius and Millard answered, 'It's not ambition, Ric, it's gratitude that makes life meaningful.' And he offered to paint the cover for one of Ric's books of poetry. And Ric, on the spot, offered to read Millard and his wife Mary, and all of us there his latest batch of poems. This story touches me deeply because Millard Sheets is my wife's father."

Tom also recalls a very powerful first meeting with Ric: "Rev. Brandoch Lovely at the Neighborhood Church in Pasadena, where I was the Assistant Minister, asked me to escort Ric to Pasadena City College where he was doing a poetry reading. It was 1970 and I was a newbie to the UU ministry. The reading took place in a noisy room right after lunch; an almost impossible situation. But it didn't matter because when this guy read about loneliness and love I wept and wept, my tears wetting the ground and unquestionably fertilizing the rest of my ministry. I don't know what was heard by the students, but this man's soul altered the way I would do religion during my 37 years in the ministry."

Now, at the other end of his ministry, Tom gives this view: "Our families are so intertwined. Ric incorporated vignettes of his own kids' stories into his poetry, and our kids are in there too. Our now 39 year old airline pilot, Russ, is quoted as a five-year-old. So Ric and Billie Barbara are forever embedded in the innards of our children's consciousness. For them poetry begins and ends with Ric Masten. They never read Shakespeare and will likely cart both their mother's and father's sermons to the dump someday. But the poetry volumes of Ric's are precious treasures indeed. Those will be passed down to their children and their children's children."

The reader of this chapter may have noticed by now that every Masten colleague mentioned up to this point is of the male persuasion. As previously stated, that was the nature of the era being discussed. It was, with very few exceptions, the ol' boys—and the younger ol' boys in waiting—who pretty much occupied the UU ministerial territory then. Beginning in the early-to-mid 1980s, however, the ground began to move. What took place was both a gender shift and much more than a gender shift. There was an influx of women into the UU ministry; and they, in turn, redefined the nature of that ministry. There was no abrupt turning away from the intellectual humanism that had characterized Unitarian Universalism since the time of the 1961 merger. Humanism continues to be one of the more definitive strands in UUism today; and we certainly haven't become anti-intellectuals.

But matters of the heart and soul—as well as the mind—began to get more attention in our worship and in congregational life. The pursuit of spirituality, that is to say the search for a sense of connection and relationship with a Presence or Power greater than oneself, has become accepted and encouraged in UU circles in ways that it previously had not. The fact that these changes began to take place at the same time that an influx of women began entering the Unitarian Universalist ministry is not a coincidence.

Change, of course, brings resistance, even on the part of the supposedly "enlightened." Some of the ol' boys didn't like the feel of the tectonic plates shifting beneath their feet. It made them feel nervous and threatened. Ric was perceptive enough to see what was happening, on the human level, to some of his colleagues; and he wrote about it in his poem *Oratorus Rex!*

Reading this poem in the year 2007 I find it more humorous than anything else; and Ric probably got a few chuckles himself as he wrote it nearly a quarter-century ago. But it has a pretty hard bite to it:

> ...
> *but in the mucky discourse*
> *that followed dinner last night*
> *the dinosaur*
> *came to the end of its reign*
>
> *there*
> *mired in a tar pit*
> *of yesterday's thinking*

THE MINISTER/POET—AS COLLEAGUE

unable to free themselves
from too much Chardonnay
they bellowed and raged—thrashing about
sawing the charged air with their teeth
bewildered—wounded—feeling betrayed
no longer influential enough
to throw their weight around
they went down slowly
glaring directly into our eyes

This is tough stuff, and there may have been at least some measure of retribution behind these words. They were written after a UU ministers' chapter gathering at which Ric was feeling ostracized, and had witnessed a similar kind of ostracizing being directed at the only woman at the gathering, the aforementioned Rev. Carolyn Owen-Towle: "They all got drunk. Many of them had previously boycotted my appearance at the Large Church Conference in Santa Barbara. Carolyn Owen-Towle was at this meeting and they were rude to her. The good ol' boys just couldn't understand what was happening and they didn't want much to do with me."

Ric elaborates: "I was a relief from the humanist head thinking. I came in singing folk songs and reading poems. I rode in on a hunger for something other than the head. I do not call myself an atheist. I'm a non-theist, but I come in and talk about the voice of the hive—what is it that holds the bee hive together? What is it that holds the human hive together? I guess you could call it God, or whatever you want. That poem says it."

A related issue in this changing of the guard dynamic, however, was an unwillingness on the part of some ministers to show they actually were impressed by Ric for fear of how that might play in front of their other colleagues. Here's what Ric experienced both during and after a ministerial gathering conference called "Refugio" (as in seeking refuge): "Howard Matson took me to Refugio. I did my thing, sang some songs, read a few poems. When I was done they all got up and walked away without a word. I figured I'd flunked out. But later I got nine letters out of the twenty ministers that were there saying they were personally impressed and invited me to come to their churches. But they couldn't show that in front of the others. They didn't want the others to know they'd been impressed enough by me to want me in their churches—even though nearly half of them all felt the same way!"

If some of his more "elder statesmen" colleagues were not well attuned to the voice of the hive, and the yearnings of even religious liberals to hear it, Ric Masten saw it in ways that these particular colleagues of his could not. He ends his harshly worded poem on a sympathetic note towards them:

> *there is always something*
> *about a change for the better*
> *that is terribly terribly*
> *sad*

While the many colleagues with whom he did have a close and friendly relationship were men, Ric's poetic style of ministry anticipated the direction the UU ministry would take as more and more women came into it. Maybe this is why, as he observes, "I've never had a UU woman minister whom I knew turn me down for an appearance when I called. They always invited me. Now the dialogues I do, using my poems in a Sunday service are often male/female dialogues and poet/minister dialogues all at the same time."

When the church where Ric and Billie first discovered Unitarian Universalism called Rev. Elizabeth Miller to be their minister in 1997, she and Ric initiated a practice of doing a poetic dialogue sermon once a year during her nine year ministry with the Unitarian Universalist Church of the Monterey Peninsula. "Beth and I danced once a year" as Ric put it.

In the summer of 2006 Rev. Miller became the Director of the Unitarian Universalist Association's Department of Ministry and Congregational Leadership. She can now look back on the nine years when Ric was both a colleague and a member of her congregation. In a conversation about what makes the things Ric does a ministry, as compared or contrasted with simply entertainment, Beth says, "I think it is precisely the vulnerability of his poetry that makes it more than entertainment, and doing it in a church setting gives it a different quality. When he does it on a Sunday morning in a church there is an opening there that invites those in the congregation to share parts of their lives as well." Getting down to cases, Beth adds, "With the Bixby Bridge poem, people who had had experiences of suicide in their family, or who had contemplated it themselves, would frequently want to speak to Ric or speak to me about those experiences. He could offer it in a church as processed experience and not raw experience."

It's very interesting how things come round. The same poem that had some of Ric's colleagues ready to dismiss him from the ministry because of his reading it in a church setting, is now cited by another colleague some three decades later as a positive example of how he does ministry. Rev. Miller is also correct in noting that the passing of time is one of the things that has allowed this poem to become an instrument of ministry. Beth also notes, "Nothing in Ric's life is unique in and of itself. What is unique is how he expresses it and how he puts it out there in ways that touch the lives of others…I have a great deal of respect for him."

Most ministers, myself included, will tell you that among the things we value most highly in our ministries are the admiration and respect of colleagues. With these kinds of thoughts and sentiments being expressed by Rev. Miller, who is now the person—and the woman—whose job it is to attend to both the operation and the quality of the Unitarian Universalist ministry across the entire Unitarian Universalist Association, Ric Masten has certainly achieved that kind of respect and admiration.

CHAPTER EIGHT:
The Minister/Poet—Family Matters

in the driveway of a renovated apartment complex dwarfing a chair
the continent of Africa sat getting a haircut
the barber—a Latino wore soiled institutional whites
I slowed to first gear. "I'm looking for Genesis House," I said
and the haircut said: "You're here. Visitors register over there."

I followed the motion of his head to a doorway marked "Office"
a group of marginal looking people stood around it chain smoking
eyeing me suspiciously—one of them approached
"Hi Dad, I didn't think anyone would come." and why should he
considering all the years of lies and manipulation and denial
"Neither did I." I said signing in

after that it was a minefield—father and son taking up positions
at opposite ends of the dusty old couch that sat outside the courtyard
gingerly stepping around the dangerous ground
avoiding the obvious trip wires—sticking to safe subjects
I held my tongue determined not to set him off or blow up myself
perhaps later in the recovery we can sweep the relationship clean
digging up and disarming the booby traps
but for now to survive the war even for a short visit
would be more than enough

getting up to go I told him about how much we enjoyed taking care
of his son Little Ricky and about waiting at the mailboxes each day
to meet the carpool sadly adding the grim footnote that when he was
   a boy
coming home from school I can't remember ever doing as much for
   him
"Well, you did today, Dad."
as I left I looked back and was surprised to see the haircut
and some of the other residents waving—as if I were family
which of course I was

Genesis House by Ric Masten

The above poem is a snapshot. Like most snapshots it offers a glimpse of truth; the key word, of course, being glimpse. To read it is to be touched by the description of what has to be a painful father and son visit. The visit concludes on a "grim footnote" of self-recrimination on the part of the father, as he admonishes himself for not having devoted the time to his son that he devoted to the sons of his son, whom he and his wife helped raise. Here is Ric Masten, the father and grandfather, offering up another piece of his life through his poetry. But it's a glimpse, a snapshot.

There's another snapshot—a literal one this time. It is a family photo of the Mastens found in the biographical introduction to a retrospective of Ric's work, published in 2000, titled *Let It Be a Dance— Words and One Liners* (Sun-Ink Presentations). There they are: Ric and Billie Barbara along with daughters Ellen, April, and Jerri, and son Stuart, all smiles and sweetness. Stuart's smile looks a bit forced, but it's there. Even the author of the bio piece, Vincent DiGirolamo, is family. He's April's husband and Ric and Billie's son-in-law.

I'm guessing there's a zone somewhere between that picture and the *Genesis House* poem where one finds the real life story of the

Mastens. It is the same zone that exists for most families, actually. It's the zone between their picture-ideal and the real world dynamics which practically all families have to deal with.

Seeing the Masten family photo recalls a passage in Jack Kerouac's *On the Road* in which the novel's two central characters are looking at family pictures they have in their wallets. Kerouac, as Sal Paradise, muses: "I realized these were all the snapshots which our children would look at someday with wonder, thinking their parents had lived smooth, well-ordered, and stabilized-within-the-photo lives and got up in the morning to walk proudly on the sidewalks of life, never dreaming the raggedy madness and riot of our actual lives." Kerouac is identifying a universal breech. It is the breech between the life we present to the world, and the life best known to us that we carry forth from day-to-day and year-to-year with its occasions of "raggedy madness and riot."

Ministers, especially those who are raising families, know about this breech all too well. There is the life you present to those with whom you minister, and then there's the life that is known to your spouse, children, in-laws, siblings, and the like. It's not that one life is "phony" and the other "real." Each one has a reality of its own. But there are lines, however fuzzy, that run between them. One of the many challenges of ministry is determining how much of his or her family life a minister brings into ministry itself. It is one more variation, really, on the larger question and challenge of how much of a minister's humanity does s/he expose in the all-too-human enterprise of ministry.

The question and challenge become all the more pointed when one is wearing the hats of minister and poet at the same time, as Ric Masten does. Poets stand naked while ministers are expected to, and indeed are counseled to, maintain certain prudent boundaries between their public and private selves. As a troubadour minister, Ric has crossed and navigated those boundaries in ways that his colleagues in more traditional forms of ministry usually cannot. I regard this ability and proclivity of Ric's as part of his gift to our liberal religious movement, whether or not that gift has been well received at times. Fool or not, Ric the poet can rush in to places where his more settled colleagues dare not tread.

Here's two more snapshots. The first is a loving tribute from Ric's youngest daughter, Ellen. The title is straightforward enough:

TO MY DAD

*I have spent my life among
weavers of words
spinning their colorful lines
of poetry
on the great loom of life*

*looking back to see what they have spun
and to explore the patterns they made
along the way*

*for an unexamined life is not worth
weaving
or perhaps
an unlived life is not worth examining*

*so let the poets weave
and I will just strive to live*

Intended or not, the last two lines are as revealing as the scene described in *Genesis House*. Ric wove his poems, and his speaking poet/troubadour life, as his family strove to live. Sometimes they lived with him and sometimes without him.

Still another snapshot poem is by Stuart himself. It's his take on the Genesis House setting. He simply titles it:

GH

It is cold
And it is dark inside of me
But the room is light and warm

I'm having trouble with the women
In the GH today
Pushing—shoving me
Taking me back till I feel cornered
Till I feel lost

Joan, a counselor
Sat down directly in front of me
"Simply a guide," as she liked to say
"Picture your father. What do you see?"

An image took Joan's place
In the chair before me
My father faint and hollow

"He's empty," I said

Joan said, "He didn't protect you
From your relatives, did he?"

"No." I said.

"Time to heal! Time to let go of the past!"

At that moment I feel a physical snap inside
A sudden release at her words
My dad growing solid before my eyes

Sitting there large as life in my mind
And I think he smiled

"What do you feel?"

"My father is whole again
And I feel I can love him again."

Silently I whispered, "I love you Dad."

Ric asked Stuart to contribute this poem for the weekly Words and One-Liners he (Ric) posts on his website, with the wry observation that he even paid his son $50.00 for it. In introducing the poem Ric comments, "When Stuart was growing up I was an absentee father chasing my folk-singing dream around the country and down the road. I was never there when Stuart might have wanted or needed his old man to be there for him. He found another father figure—one of our fast and loose neighbors who was not the best role model in the world. No doubt the drug problem really began there."

The absence of a parent, of course, does not affect all of his or her offspring in the same way. Ric's daughters are each making a good life of it with careers, interests, and families of their own. But their father's absence was felt by all of them. Daughter Jerri recalls: "Dad was always on the road. For the main part of my childhood he was home for a couple of months and then gone for a couple of months and on like that. We really weren't aware of how his absence was affecting us when it was going on. It's only in the last few years that he's focused on the absent parent part of his life and career."

Writing out of both his absence from them and his presence with them, Ric makes his family very much a part of the fabric of his poetry. The joy and love of family life are interwoven, in Kerouac's language, with the raggedy madness and riot of it all. To lay it out in very broad, and sometimes overlapping categories, Ric has written Mother poems, Kids poems, Grandkids poems, and Billie Barbara poems.

As Vincent DiGirolamo puts it in the biographical sketch cited earlier, Ric experienced his mother, Hildreth Masten Hare, as "both neglectful and domineering." As noted in Chapter Two, Ric's father, Richard T. Masten, died when Ric was 12 and Hildreth remarried Chester Hare, an optometrist. Hildreth and Chester continued to raise Ric and his younger brother and sister. One outcome of this upbringing was that Ric was left with a hefty repository of "mommy issues."

If a picture paints a thousand words, a well written poem can convey a life-time of thought, feeling, and emotion. The first two stanzas of Ric's *Mother's Voice as Part of the Estate*, written following his mother's death, do just that:

> *thank god*
> *it wasn't me she doted on*
> *otherwise I'd have been the one*
> *chosen to inherit Birdy*
> *mother's irksome parrot*
> *that dubious honor was bequeathed*
> *to her youngest son—the pet*
> *the one who could always get*
> *his way with the queen—*
> *got it in the end—*
> *the talking albatross I mean*
>
> *the rest of us stifling a grin*
> *as we watched the two of them begin*
> *an ephemeral relationship*
> *that didn't make it through the fall*
> *but then*
> *I doubt if anyone could live*
> *with the disembodied voice*

> *still calling his name*
> *"Donn!"*
> *still ruling the roost*
> *cigarette hack and all.*

It is, in fact, when Ric reflects upon the effect his mother had on him that he sees how that effect played out in how he dealt with his own children: "How would you like to have a father who, in the name of poetry and art, hung out the family laundry for all to see? 'Grist for the mill,' was my standard excuse. And I should have known better having had a very funny mother who held court every afternoon at the local watering hole telling side splitting tales about me and my siblings. It has taken me a long while to forgive her for that."

Again, daughter Jerri observes, "Dad was not able to own what his part in our dysfunction was about. Now he is able to own it, but not while it was going on. Now he has made some amends about it."

In another verse of the previously cited *Notice Me!* Ric assumes, or imagines, the viewpoint of one—or maybe its a combination—of his children as they experienced him and the adults around him:

> *we can't be bothered now*
> *the distant voices said*
> *when I came to share*
> *the butterfly I found*
> *and I'd look up into the nostrils*
> *of the faces overhead*
> *but I never caught the giants*
> *lookin' down*
>
> *yeah, I'm the poor misshapen figure*
> *in the backroom of your home*
> *your little baby's gone*
> *and blown his mind*

he's at the nursery window
standin' all alone
trying to catch the eye
of the blind...

Then there's this one written for his daughter Ellen, and given that title as well:

ELLEN

my youngest daughter
likes to ride
to the mailbox with me

she fetches the mail
while I turn the car around
then she climbs into the back seat

and doles out my letters
slowly
inspecting each envelope

till I am infuriated
and turn red
and shout at her

Ellen!
gimme
the letters!

my youngest daughter likes to do this
it is one of the few times
she has my full attention

Then, over the years, the struggles, the missteps, and, yes, the delights of parenthood give way to the not-so-encumbered delights of grandparenthood. Although, as alluded to in *Genesis House*, some parenting duties did come to be taken on by the grandparents. Ric and Billie have five grandchildren altogether. Gaia is the daughter of Ellen. Taylor and Ricky are Stuart's sons. Cara is April's daughter. Nathan is Jerri's son. They are all now in their late teens or young adulthood. Each and all of them have found their way into the Ric Masten *oeuvre*.

The cover of *Notice Me!* is adorned by a four year old Nathan Masten's painting of a flower growing in the midst of blades of grass. The painting is one that most proud grandparents would put on their refrigerator with magnets. Ric puts it on the cover of a collection of his poems.

One of Ric's more poignant grandchildren poems describes a building project undertaken by two of his granddaughters, Cara and Gaia, during a stay at their grandparent's Palo Colorado home. Recalling the event, Ric is left wondering about some of his own motivations:

PONY ISLAND

submerged in sadness
I acknowledge the relentless
passage of time
Pony Island is gone
and oddly the demolition was done by me
I say oddly
because from the nineteenth of July
to the twelfth of August
I watched entranced
while my visiting granddaughters
worked the fantasy out in the dirt driveway
below my writing-room window

Cara

the solemn nine-year-old bossing the job
with Gaia—a lively firecracker five
taken on as the tireless "go fer"
the two of them spending
the long summer afternoons
raiding the wood box
pilfering rocks from the garden walls
sneaking my tools out of the shop
digging and scraping
shaping the pliable surface
into every little girl's
enchanted sandbox dream

barn and stables
paddock and polo field
a steeplechase—a race track
pastures—pond and stream
all of this surrounded by bright blue water
an equestrian Bali Ha'i
set in the center of a make-believe sea
"Pony Island!" Cara proclaimed as Gaia
meticulously—breathlessly—endlessly
explained the intricate topography

but as previously revealed
this enchanted domain is no more
because for reasons I have yet to understand
the moment I returned home from the airport
I went with shovel and rake in hand
directly to the now abandoned building site
and almost without thinking
strangely driven –a man possessed

I thoroughly policed the area
returning blocks and sticks
to the wood box
filling in ditches furrows and holes
removing
the carefully placed rocks and twigs
raking and watering
until there was nothing left—nothing

except the awful melancholy inside
at the center—like an island
and the sound of hoof beats racing off
down a deserted beach
disappearing the way time does

At one point Ric and Billie Barbara became the *de facto* parents to their grandsons from Stuart's marriage. This portion of *Suddenly Grandsons* is Ric's poetic rendition of that experience:

the orphans of dysfunction
appear on our doorstep...
coming to us
through the auspices of a marriage
dismantled by codependence
and substance abuse
Mommy
dwindling down to a few elusive
calls from the East
Dad
unraveling locally
looking in taprooms for self-esteem
counseling with barkeeps
hard-pressed to find time

for the traditional
good night boys
sweet dreams
and don't let the bedbugs bite

sadly

at this juncture
there is no light at the end of the tunnel
just the stunning enormity of recent events
the night tear-streaked at first
Grandma punishing her pillow with a fist
damn it
I've already done this!
I'm not a child- rearing machine
life must be more
than picking toys up off the floor
more than making boys make beds
being resented and unappreciated
(then the saving grace of laughter)
that is until after
one of them becomes a famous author
and like Truman Capote
pens a moving
childhood remembrance of me...
of course by then I'll be dead

for Gramps an opposite reaction
here was an opportunity
to beat myself black and blue
building forts—hanging swings
doing things
I didn't do the first time around

...
Gramps and Grandma
are doing as well as can be expected
valiantly trying not to forget
that these dear little troopers
really don't belong to us
and that like it or not
the future depends entirely
upon the action and reaction
of two loose cannons

For all the pages of Mom, Kids, and Grandkids poems Ric has written and read to his audiences over the years and decades, the best known collection—with accompanying commentary—of family matters poems are the ones he and Billie Barbara co-authored under the title *His and Hers.* The physical copies of this work—ones you can hold in your hand—are long out of print. But they continue to be produced on home and office printers across the land more than thirty years after they were originally written thanks to a link on Ric's website.

There are any number of ways into the *His and Hers* story. This is an account of how Rev. Rolfe Gerhart, now in retirement, stumbled across it. A very skilled guitar and mandolin maker, Rolfe was innocently trying to figure out how to get a guitar he'd made for Ric to him when he ran head-on into a not-so-innocent situation:

"The guitar was finished just before the 1973 General Assembly. in Toronto and I said I'd give it to Ric there. Then I found out I couldn't take the guitar to Canada and deliver it commercially and have him take it home. So I called Billie in Big Sur to see how I could reach Ric and arrange for him to get the guitar. Billie said he was in Chicago and gave me a number to reach him there. So I called the number and a woman answered, and I asked if Ric was there. She asked how I knew he was there, and I said I'd gotten the number from Billie. She said, "Ohhh..."

"She did a quick recovery and said she'd get in touch with Ric and have him call me. Ric did call me back and we arranged for me to ship the guitar to him at one of the Chicago airports. I didn't know what was going on. Later I found out Ric was having an affair with this woman, and she didn't know Bille knew about it. Billie was having an affair of her own with a millionaire. Ric later said that when he left the house in Chicago he decided he would end it, and that's how they got into the whole *His and Her* thing and the contract and all that."

Whatever his counter-cultural affectations may have been—running off to Big Sur "to do a hippie kind of thing with a bone around my neck" as he put it—Ric and Billie Barbara had largely internalized, consciously or not, the mainstream cultural notions of what a marriage in 1950s America was supposed to be. The woman stayed home to tend the house and raise the kids while the man went forth to pursue a career. While the career Ric was pursuing may have been offbeat for the times, the gender roles he and Billie assumed were classic 1950s Americana, with the wife taking the lion's (lioness'?) share of her identity from her husband.

Ric and Billie Barbara first met when Ric, with a couple of partners, was trying to launch a local theater company in Carmel and Billie tried out for one of the plays they were producing. Billie still shows a girl-like smile when she recalls their first meeting: "When I first saw Ric I saw a combination of Shakespeare and Jesus, my first two loves." And she got her own taste of family matters early on: "I was the one who first suggested we get married, and Ric said, 'I'll have to ask my mother first.'" [Big laugh!] Billie does give her mother-in-law credit where it's due, however: "She (Ric's mother) was very good for me because she got me into AA with her; and that's been important because I've been in AA ever since."

That was the beginning. And so it went for some 20 years of conventional marriage, albeit with Ric's unconventional ministry. Then it took this turn, as Ric poetically describes in these lines from *The*

Creative Divorce Set-Up:

*the nesting marriage over
the youngest bird ready to fly
both my wife Billie Barbara and I
after twenty years of fidelity
amazingly, within 11 days of each other
and unbeknown to each other
broke the vows
she with an artist while I was on the road
and I with a young career woman in the Midwest.*

*the comical night that it all came to light
found us unable to be angry
with each other
I mean how can you get mad at someone
for doing the same thing you've been doing...
you can!*

*so we sat on the edge of the bed
comparing notes
laughing
and wondering where our own relationship
had gone sour*

...

*I had become the maintenance man
to Billie Barbara
and she the big nurse to me
but talking through the night we realized
that there was an undeniable closeness between us
resting on things*

like waiting in hospital halls
to learn whether our son would die
after the motorcycle wreck
and yet, undeniably our new loves
had filled us with a zest that we had lost
somewhere in the maze
of everyday living.

Bille Barbara, of course, had her own version as well:

WAITING

And I have waited
I waited to grow up—use lipstick
To be kissed, to wear a bra,
For my Prince to come, to vote.
I waited for some man
To ask me to marry him
And have children
I waited in line for stamps
And groceries
In lobbies for movies
In parked cars for children at lessons
For airplanes to come bringing you in
For airplanes to go taking you out
I waited for the roast to get done,
The jello to set, the light to turn green
Waiting to move on,
To go away on vacations
And to go back home
The children grew up
And my hair is turning grey

And I have waited
For you to ask me to speak for myself

Hey! It's my turn
I will speak for myself

And speak she does, in this one:

CELEBRATION
I celebrate myself
The woman
The true woman
Not assumed
Not to be taken away
Billie Barbara
That is Billie Barbara
That is Billie Barbara
I am
An energy event!

This is just a slice of the poetry found in the book *His and Hers: A Voyage Through the Middle Age Crazies* that Ric and Billie Barbara wrote in the aftermath of the discovery of their respective affairs, to tell how they re-worked their marriage altogether. The book concludes with the contract they wrote—a re-negotiated marriage agreement—as a re-starting of their marriage. Each year since 1974, on September 3, they re-enact a "divorce" and a "re-marriage" (sans legalities) and recommit themselves to another year of relationship. They call it "The Mastens' Annual Relationship Renewal." It seems to be working.

[Note: For those readers who would like to peruse the entire text, *His and Hers* is on-line at www.ric-masten.net. When the homepage comes up, click on "His and Hers" and it's all there.]

One of the more significant changes in their shared life following the writing of *His and Hers* was that Ric and Billie Barbara began touring together, taking their book and their story on the road. They did much of their travels in a van called *The Homesick Snail*, the title of one of Ric's children's poems. With a certain ruefulness, Ric recalls those days:

"Talk about scaring people to death! Ric Masten and his wife are coming to town! Hot damn! And they'd all come down, and we'd do the "His and Her" program. It would start out funny about husband/wife things and then all of a sudden it would be about an affair. And you could see the women looking up at their husbands. In a way it was unfair because they had come to hear this folksinger and poet, and then they were in the throes of an affair. But it had a happy ending as we told of how we found a way to know each other again and signed a yearly contract. Instead of getting divorced like most normal people we wrote a bunch of poems, put them in a book, and took it on the road."

Backing up a bit, Ric continues:

"Here I'd been running around telling all these ministers, 'Can't you keep it in your pants?' This was the 70's when a lot of that was going on. The joke line going around then was be at least 50 miles from your home if you're having an affair, and 75 miles if it's with a goat! And then I got into a mess of my own. What it was with me was the middle age crazies. It was that time for me. But I knew I didn't want to leave Billie, and so we sat down together and wrote *His and Hers* and then went on the road with it."

Elaborating on the book's sub-title Ric describes the middle-age crazies in this way: "To me the middle-age crazies are when you get to be around 50 or 60. It's especially true for men who are linear, and for linear women as well. You begin to say, 'I've only got one more chance for one more change.' This is when electrical engineers go to Starr King to become ministers. A lot of divorces happen here, too. You reach the point where you ask yourself if there's more to life than what you're doing. So in these middle-age crazies we do go a little crazy and do strange things. But I knew I didn't want to spend the rest of my life with that woman in Rockford, Illinois. It was the middle age crazies."

With the middle-age crazies successfully navigated, Ric and Billie Barbara enjoy some of the ongoing rewards of family life at this point in their lives. They and their daughters occasionally share in performances when they are able to be together in the same place at the same time. Rosemary Matson sees it this way: "For years Ric dominated the scene. His daughters and his wife were equally talented, but he was the one who got all the attention. He was the coffee table dancer and they were just there. But they could sing too, and write poetry (and) when the women began to come out the whole family would perform."

True to Rosemary's observations, in the years—and now decades—since *His and Hers* Billie Barbara, and Jerri, April, and Ellen, have each created strong and vibrant identities of their own. Jerraldine lives with her husband Christian Hanson on her parent's property in Big Sur where she pursues her career as an artist, photographer, and poet. She also performs marriages with an earth-based ceremony. "I use a marrying blanket," she explains, "And I do them with a friend, Daniel Spinning-Wind, a local O'holone Indian. He also plays drums in the background when I read my poems." With a wry smile Jerri adds, "I've wanted to keep my own talents small as I've had divas for parents." Jerri and Christian's son, Nathan, also lives nearby and sometimes accompanies Ric on his travels as his grandfather's roadie.

April is married, as noted, to Vincent DiGirolamo. They have one daughter, Cara, and also helped to raise Ricky, Stuart's youngest son. April is a history professor at the State University of New York at Stony Brook. She writes about the relationship between political economies and the visual and performing arts.

Ellen lives in Santa Cruz, California with her daughter Gaia, and husband, Thomas Hunt. After years of teaching she is now a counselor. Billie Barbara, who at times was responsible for raising Stuart's boys, also has a well established local—and beyond—reputation as a poet and artist in her own right.

In the course of this writing Stuart has re-connected with his parents in some very significant ways, and has even become his father's roadie on some of Ric's closer to home gigs in central California. As Stuart puts it, he has "recently returned from that land beyond reality." These words are in a poem where Stuart describes his return after being among what he calls "the living dead," and a conversation it prompted while recently accompanying Ric on a reading:

THE OTHER UNIVERSE

"Where have you been?"
An ex-Unitarian minister inquired
Last Sunday at Dad's reading.

"I've been in another universe."
"You have?" he asked, "What do you mean?"
I smiled because only a Unitarian
Would be curious about such things.
"I've been among the living dead."
He smiled knowingly—"I had a sister once,"
He said thoughtfully,
The pure light of unconditional love
Occupied his eyes.

I nodded, "It is hard to put closure
On an association one has had
With the living dead.
A girlfriend, family member, friend or wife
Caught up in a relationship gone bad.
Just count your losses and walk away,
Shed a tear and get on with your life.

But how do we mourn the living dead?
There is no finality.

And I know, having recently returned
From that land beyond reality,
A place where love, money, and family
Have no meaning
Save the opportunity for enablement."
The man nodded sadly.

"Love is an enduring thing," I said.
"Mourn her loss
And let there be closure as you await
Her resurrection through recovery
Or until she is actually dead.
But keep a wary eye, my friend, it is better
To let go and wail than die slowly with her
Before your time."

We shook hands
No more was needed to be said.

In order to successfully pursue any number of careers, one must learn the craft and deal with the perils of being a public person. Being a minister, poet, politician, performer—to name just a few—require a person to don a public persona. Behind that public persona, of course, is the whole mish-mash of a much more personal and private life. Ministers, performers, and politicians (to name but three) all have their publics, who want to know who they "really are." It's an exquisitely fine line a public person walks between demonstrating personal authenticity and respecting the privacy of his/her family life. As a poet, performer, and troubadour minister Ric Masten has had his public, and his public persona, for nearly all of his adult life. He has chosen to make much of his family life—with its pains and its joys—a part of that public persona.

My purpose is not to pass judgment on Ric's choices as to how much he exposed of his family life. His choices stand on their own. I would suggest that those who engage in ministry, or whose career requires of them any kind of a public life, that they use Ric's choices as a marker in determining how much of your private self you bring to your public persona. His choices may not be yours, but perhaps they can be of help in dealing with such questions as these:

How do you honestly share and expose your humanity, while still keeping some of your all-too-human characteristics for yourself and for those you love the most? How do you convey your love and care for your family without inadvertently hurting them? How do you characterize your family members at certain phases of their lives while also leaving them the space to change and grow? These are among the many balancing acts that all persons who have to attend to their public and private lives deal with—ministers certainly included.

In the end, love may not conquer all but it does have an amazing resiliency when it comes to the many trials and tests of family matters. On the portion of Ric's website that his daughter Jerraldine occupies is a very personal tribute to her father that shows both her love for him and her awareness that no relationship is forever. While the words are Jerri's the sentiments they convey most certainly go well beyond her.

DADDY, WALK WITH ME

Daddy, I wish you could get up and walk with me
Take my hand—my strength
We'll fly over the canyons and mountains
Leave behind sickness and pain
Soar with the hawks
Hovering over Pico Blanco and Bixby
The bridges and beaches of my childhood
Let's close our eyes, Dad, and go there now
Before you fly off on your own
And leave me here with your old sweaters and books.
I can't touch your hand

I can only find you in the dark
In my dreams as I sleep on piles of warm cardigans
And poems and pictures
Your paintings of familiar places
Family outings—memories of long ago.

CHAPTER NINE:

"The Ministry For Which I've Been Preparing All My Life"

in my early twenties
I went along with Dylan Thomas
boasting that I wanted to go out
not gently but raging
shaking my fist
staring death down

however this daring statement
was somewhat revised
when in my forties I realized
that death does the staring
I do the down

so I began hoping
it would happen to me
like it happened to the sentry
in all those
John Wayne Fort Apache movies
found dead in the morning
face down—an arrow in the back
"Poor Devil,"
the Sergeant always said
"Never knew what hit him."

at the time I liked that—
the end taking me
completely by surprise
the bravado left in the hands
of a hard drinking Welshman
still wet behind the ears

older and wiser now
over seventy
and with a terminal disease
the only thing right about
what the Sergeant said
was the "Poor Devil" part

"Poor devil"
never used an opening
to tell loved ones he loved them
never seized the opportunity
to give praise for the sunrise
or drink in a sunset
moment after moment
passing him by
while he marched through life
staring straight ahead
believing in tomorrow
"Poor Devil!"

how much fuller
richer and pleasing life becomes
when you are lucky enough
to see the arrow coming

"Poor Devil!" by Ric Masten

Except for our brief meet-up in 1991 I've only known Ric Masten since he's seen the arrow coming. We work on this book even as the arrow is in flight; and we work against a deadline in the most literal sense of the word. Well, yes, philosophically speaking the arrow that finally gets us is released the moment we're born; and each and every thing we do with every moment of our lives is done in the face of an approaching ultimate deadline. But just as an imminent execution concentrates the mind of the condemned, a diagnosis of terminal cancer takes that flippantly expressed line about how "we all gotta go sometime" straight out of the esoteric air and puts it smack on the ground.

For Ric Masten, we-all-gotta-go-sometime hit the ground in February of 1999 when he was diagnosed with incurable advanced metastic prostate cancer. He first thought he'd just experienced a groin pull when he went up a ladder to do some home repair the month prior. But the pain persisted, and one test and examination led to another, and what eventually came up was the "Big C."

The term "incurable" did not mean—and has not meant—immediately terminal. Instead, this diagnosis has brought yet another dimension to Ric's ministry over the past 7 to 8 years that has had an impact both within and far beyond the Unitarian Universalist community. Indeed, following his appearance, in 2005, before a convention of the National Prostate Cancer Coalition in Washington, D.C. the organization dubbed Ric the "Poet Laureate of Prostate Cancer."

Ric's response to his cancer has fit quite consistently, in fact, into his larger life pattern. Just as a jeopardized marriage led to his and Billie's *His and Her* poems, and a pass at suicide yielded *The Bixby Bridge Incident*, and the Masten family dynamics have been given their numerous poetic expressions over the years, the past 7-8 years have seen a collection of cancer survivor—or "cancer combatant" as Ric prefers—poems come to characterize his writing. Keeping in character, Ric's wide-open willingness to share his dealings with his diagnosis—with the usual Masten blend of humor and poignancy—has touched and opened up many other men and their families all around the country who are dealing with the same ominous stuff.

One example of this occurred just a few months after the initial cancer diagnosis in April of 1999: "I did a program for the Unitarian Society of Livermore. About 60 people. I had a bet with the fellow who introduced me, that at least seven out of the 60 would come up after the reading (which would include my recent prostate musings) and share a personal war story about prostate cancer. I was right. Exactly seven approached with an encouraging tale about themselves, or a husband, or a brother, or a son." Then came the twist of humor: "I was told to prepare myself for hot flashes and water retention, to which Billie Barbara said, 'Join the club!'" And if that weren't enough, Ric ends the story on this note: "I ended my presentation with one of those inspirational poetic moments, a hot flash if you will. 'It just occurred to me,' I said, 'I'm going to get rich selling a bumper sticker I just thought of—REAL MEN DON'T NEED BALLS.'"

So, the magical ministry goes on. Ric's on the road schedule is not as heavy as it once was, but the on-line ministry he has developed by way of the Prostate Cancer Odyssey section of his website has reached thousands of cancer survivor/combatants and their families since he began it in 1999 shortly after the initial diagnosis came down. The above story is but one of the numerous tales Ric offers in his odyssey, along with the accounts—the literal ups and downs of PSA numbers—included as well. These lines capture well the spirit of his on-line ministry and sharing, and what it does for him as well as for those he reaches out to:

IN SUPPORT OF SUPPORT GROUPS

I wonder where I'd be without the Internet
and the parade of dear supportive spirits
met there in cyberspace
that mystical place where aid
care and concern are not determined

by age, gender, race, physical appearance,
economic situation or geographical location

and this
from a die-hard like me
who not ten years ago
held the computer in great disdain
convinced that poetry should be composed
on the back of an envelope
with a blunt pencil while riding on a train.

thank god I'm past these prejudices
I doubt if this recent flare-up
could have been withstood
how terrifying—
the thought of being at my writing desk
disconnected—alone
typing out memos to myself
on my dead father's ancient Underwood

Ric also sees the congruity with the life he'd been living up until 1999 and where it has gone since then: "I got terminal cancer and came to see that my whole life was a preparation for the ministry I'm doing now. It is not necessarily with the Unitarian Universalists, although they are involved. But in my on-line presence I've taken on a much wider ministry. One of the ways I'd learned to be a minister was in ministering to other UU ministers who had nobody to express their stuff to. And now I've learned to work with people who really know they're going to die. We are a culture, including UUs, who know we're going to die but don't really believe it. But people who have cancer, or a life-threatening disease—they really believe it."

Even when you do come to believe it, you still have to deal with the physical, mental, emotional, and spiritual challenges a cancer diagnosis brings. On top of all that there's the more down-to-earth matter of how to pay for treatment—especially the medications that medical insurance doesn't always cover. One way Ric put a dent in these kinds of costs was to publish, and promote among his wide constituency, the sale of a couple of coffee table books (by the Coffee Table Dancer?) of his work over the course of his career. Calling them *Ric Masten's Greatest Hits* would have been a bit crass, so they're titled *Let It Be A Dance—Words and One Liners*, published in 2002, and followed up with *Words and One Liners, Take 2*, published in 2005.

The term "one-liner" refers to the pencil drawings Ric does to accompany each poem. Each drawing is a single, unbroken line that forms a picture, or a visual representation, of the poem on the opposite page. Maybe it was for this that Ric's mother sent him to art school in Paris a half-century ago!

The two books are beautifully done, and each contains a section of poems written in the aftermath of his cancer diagnosis. In a series of prose musings that lead up to the cancer poems in the first volume Ric writes, "Hell, I've lived 70 years already—done exactly what I wanted to do with my life. All worthwhile dreams have come true. All things considered I've been truly blessed and whether my departure date is next year or 15 years from now, I'm determined not to wreck my life by doing a lousy job with my death." Then before launching into the poetry part of this section he says, "From here on, I'll let the poems document the part of the journey that brings us up to the present. A place where I can honestly say that I have been blessed, not cursed— that spiritually speaking the best thing that has ever happened to me is metastatic hormone refractory advanced prostate cancer." The poetry takes it from there.

The poems include those that are unflinchingly and excruciatingly descriptive, like the following:

DIGITAL EXAM

digital was such a sanitary hi-tech word
that is until my urologist sneaks up from behind
and gives me the bird

There are others that describe the emotional ups and downs involved in facing the next test and diagnosis:

PSA DREAD

the battle
with the "Big C" monster
is scored by the numbers
like a jury trial
digits sequester and deliberate
under a microscope the blood I bled
is analyzed—the evidence scrutinized
the side-effect of these proceedings
PSA dread

Like the aforementioned *In Support of Support Groups* there is another set of poems that point to the need to reach beyond oneself in coping with PSA dread, in order to both give and receive support and counsel. This one describes Ric's first attempt to reach out while still in the throes of the aftershocks from his initial diagnosis, when all he wanted to do, was run and, ostrich like, hide his head in the sand:

THE OSTRICH

so I go on line where dumb luck
and a benevolent "search engine"
find the Prostate Cancer Research Institute
I dial the "helpline"
and for more than an hour

an anonymous Good Samaritan
calmly slows me down until
my philosophy of life can catch up
and begin to see me through

There are a set of poems that draw on those times when Ric's philosophy of life did catch up with him, and allowed him to be in a more reflective mode. The poem *A Word for Survival* is dedicated to William Hoyt, Jr. The word, which has become Ric's watchword for living, is "spiritude."

A WORD FOR SURVIVAL

The man who coined the word
Had a terminal disease
A realist who knew that language
Strengthens, heals, and frees
Fear—the silent assassin
Will bring you to your knees
While faith can pull Excalibur
From stubborn stones with ease

The outcome of any illness
Is never absolute
No matter what the odds are
The end is always moot
It's only in uncertainty
That true hope can be found
And you can bet a sure thing
Will always let you down

He fought the "Big C" monster
With spunk and attitude
Another cockeyed optimist

You shoud not conclude
So like the fallen colors
I've taken up his word
And shout it from the hill top
Till the echo can be heard

He was no pollyanna
His word no platitude
To things considered saccharine
He could be abrupt and rude
In the present-day vernacular
He was a righteous dude
Let's hear it for the man
Who coined the word
Spiritude!

Since these poems are being written by Ric Masten, there are bound to be some playful ones as well. Facing hip replacement surgery, for example, moved him to write *On Becoming An Artificial Hipster*. The best of the playful cancer poems (if such can be imagined) is one called *The House of Drips*. In it he likens a series of chemotherapy treatments to a series of trips to a brothel, where he awaits his appointment wondering who he'll get this time around:

gathered in the parlor
beauties one and all
and I never know which cutie
will lead me down the hall
but it really doesn't matter
all are deft at what they do
so let the act of drawing straws
determine
who accesses who

After describing the various individual qualities and attributes of Vivian, Allison, Nora, and Lindy, Ric concludes on this note:

> *I call*
> *and make appointments*
> *like every other John*
> *it's to the House of Drips I go*
> *each week to get it on*
> *with four oncology nurses*
> *Yes, that's what this is about*
> *the four angels of mercy*
> *I cannot live without*

Such are the cancer poems of Ric Masten. They offer a special kind of healing language for those dealing with cancer as well as for the families, friends, and loved ones of cancer fighters. The healing effects of Ric's cancer poems and his ongoing Prostate Cancer Odyssey on his website have been felt, quite literally, worldwide. On a day in late January of 2007, during a visit with him to work on this book, he got this note from France that was signed "Mes best regards—Francoise":

"Hello Ric—I discovered your 'Odyssey' only yesterday. I have been dealing with my husband's disease for a year now, and to see your long battle which has been going on for 9 years is a beam of light. My husband was diagnosed a year ago at age 61 with a PSA of 156 and metastases on his bones right from the start. I find it funny when you mention the ostrich because I think my husband is really acting like that too. He relies totally on me for all medical information. He prefers to work in his job as much as before and has his pride in hiding his disease from anyone as long as his physical appearance is not too damaged. He prefers not to hear too much about cancer; that is a word he would like to forget!"

Then Francoise concludes, "Not only is it helpful for your own sake to write about your odyssey (probably a therapy in itself), but be aware that it brings some answers and hope to other patients who happen to read you."

Right around the same time as the above came Ric's way, he heard from a long-time fan who had first seen and heard him as a child, and then rediscovered him through the website: "I'm writing from Orlando, Florida. My Mom and I were e-mailing about you and *The Homesick Snail* this week when she mentioned your website. I was telling her that I intended to play your album which I've kept since you performed at the Unitarian Church in Orlando back in the 70s. I am so sorry to read about your struggles these past several years. What instantly comes to mind is what a wonderful gift and teacher you were to me as a child. You've written about your latest appointment, and I'm sorry the news was not better. I will send you my love and healing energy. May 2007 bring you good health, passionate spirit, great love, beautiful inspiration, and a deep comfort of the soul."

Weighing in on how it has been for him to put his cancer odyssey out for all to see, Ric offers this: "I've done a lot of support groups. From being on line I get about five phone calls and 20 e-mails a month from people dealing with prostate cancer. Mainly they call to be ministered to. But I'm just a fellow survivor who is willing to open up and let people into my life. After talking to a guy for an hour I hang up and then I feel better. It's selfish in a way. I feel better by talking with others."

In 2003 Ric's poetic language was placed in dialogue with the language of clinical psychology in a book he co-authored with Dr. Larry Lachman titled *Parallel Journeys*. Dr. Lachman is also a prostate cancer survivor/fighter, and is some thirty years Ric's junior. As a Clinical Psychologist he specializes in working with cancer patients and their families, and teaches psychology at the Monterey Peninsula College and John F. Kennedy University.

Ric and Larry first met in May of 2002 at a meeting of the Prostate Cancer Self-Help Group of the Central Coast at the Hospice House in Monterey. Dr. Lachman recounts it this way: "I was invited to be the lead speaker addressing the emotional and psychological challenges men face when they are diagnosed and treated for prostate cancer. On the podium Ric and I were seated by one another. And, of course, for those of you who know either Ric or me, that's like putting two 10th graders who can't stop talking in the back of the classroom. We whispered back and forth, gently elbowed one another, and traded mischievous but well intentioned humorous winks while the other panelists were speaking. From that night on, Ric and I became great friends, journeymen if you will, fellow explorers on this journey we call cancer." The book the two of them came to write is the outcome of their shared explorations.

The first thing one has to do in picking up *Parallel Journeys* is decide how to read it. The pages on the left contain Ric's poems and drawings of his prostate cancer odyssey. The pages on the right contain Dr. Lachman's writings on the psychology of cancer survival. Depending on how the reader processes the written word, one can read the pages left-to-right in tandem, or take in a run of Ric's material and then a run of Larry's. Either way the book has a decidedly unifying quality to it. Above and beyond its content it offers a good example of how the poet and the social scientist can complement one another in dealing with the same phenomenon.

Ric did not write his portion of *Parallel Journeys* with his UU minister hat on in any highly visible way. Unless you pick up the reference to "fellow clergy" in the book's Dedication, one could read this entire work and not know that "minister" is a part of Ric Masten's larger, overall persona. At the same time, one cannot come away from this book without feeling ministered to—whether it's put in those words or not. The years since 1999, in fact, offer just one of the many examples of how Ric's life and work include his troubadour minister life while also going well beyond it into much wider circles. Some of these wider circles will be further explored in the following chapter.

There is one more piece of Ric's cancer survivor/combatant life that warrants attention before moving on, however. To the yin of Ric's testimony that "spiritually speaking the best thing that ever happened to me is having advanced prostate cancer" is the yang found in his poem *Garden Pavilion*.

At one point in his cancer treatments Ric encountered a level of depression he'd never known before: "...a violent brain storm...the cranium an electric arena of unrelenting action...blackness charged with angst...unbridled thoughts stampeding..." as he puts it in *Garden Pavilion*.

This was a far cry from the low moment that had taken him to the Bixby Bridge some thirty years earlier. On that occasion he ended up thinking better of the inclinations that had drawn him there, and went back home and got on with his life instead of going over the railing. This time it was the real deal: "I was dying of cancer, my brain was full of steroids and I couldn't see clearly. I was cutting wood for the stove and figured I'd try to make it look like an accident. I wrapped the cord to my skilsaw around my foot so it would look like I'd gotten tangled up in the cord and accidentally sliced myself up with the saw. That's how I wanted it to look when Billie got home."

Suffice to say, the plan did not work as it was not fully carried forth. It came close enough, though, for his family to act:

> *at wits end my family*
> *deposits me in the Garden Pavilion*
> *an elegant name for the local loony bin*
> *I awake to walls and ceilings...*
> *three days it took to break the fall*
> *to turn around and begin the long haul out*
> *climbing up the line*
> *"better living through chemistry"*

The primary effect of this experience—this one particularly harrowing piece of his cancer odyssey—was to cause Ric to revisit and reconsider some of the judgments he'd made about those who'd taken their lives: "I realized there may well be times when one cannot go on, and I'm less critical of the real suicides." This was also one of those times when, unlike his visit to the Bixby Bridge, Ric did not have his aforementioned Observer with him. It was all very immediate as it was happening. With that realization, he writes these concluding stanzas to *Garden Pavilion*:

> *back on firmer ground I visit*
> *my own poetic archives*
> *to see what I had to say yesterday*
> *about those who gave in*
> *to depression and suicide*
>
> *and I find I have apologies to make*
> *to David "unwilling to face another day"*
> *to Ann Sexton*
> *for "going down beneath the hooves!"*
> *to Sylvia Plath who traded her bell jar*
> *for a hissing gas stove*
>
> *to Stevie Smith and John Berryman*
> *"waving—even as they fell"*
> *and to Vincent Van Gogh for falling prey*
> *to "his blinding field of hay."*
>
> *to all of you that I have criticized*
> *for taking the final step*
> *surveying it*
> *from recent lived experience*
> *my arrogant proclamations*
> *seem totally inept*

knowing what I now know
it's time to go back to the punch lines
and soften the blow

For all of his positive pronouncements about his prostate cancer journey, including his stated desire to "not wreck my life by doing a lousy job with my death," one has to appreciate Ric's honesty in relating how close he came on one occasion to deliberately taking the ultimate out. The fact that one particular turn on his now eight year journey took him into the deepest black hole of depression for a short period of time clearly sensitized Ric to the plight of others who've been there. His writing of *Garden Pavilion* is really a call for the same kind of sensitivity and empathy by those of us who cannot know what this kind of depression is like unless we've been there.

As of this writing, Ric's journey goes on. Perhaps the best way of characterizing all that this journey entails, with its many yins and yangs, is found in the poem he uses to open his section of *Parallel Journeys*:

SING A SONG

in a tiny rowboat
tryin' to cross a river
tryin' to make it to the other shore
a young man and an old man
stuck out in the middle
when a sudden storm swept away
the oars

cut off from the safety
of the solid ground they'd come from
too far to get where they longed to go
the situation was hopeless
helplessly they drifted

to the waterfall that waited
just below

like a leaf in a gutter
captured by the water
the ragin' river washing them along
they only had a moment
till they'd be carried over
so they stood up in the boat
and sang a song

sing a song
sing a song
when hope has been abandoned
sing a song
pilgrim it would be a real catastrophe
if you should fail to stand
and sing a song

crashin' through the jungle
here came this foreign feller
a hungry tiger closin' in behind
chased him to a canyon
the poor man tumbled over
but as he fell he caught a passin' vine

helplessly he dangled
while up above the tiger
settled down to play a waiting game
but the vine would never hold him
old it was and rotten
and down below another tiger came

but a berry bush was growin'
there on the bank before him
it held a single berry ripe and red
he took the tender morsel
and in the final moment
"delicious" that is what they say he said

waterfalls and tigers
somethin's gonna get ya
we're here today tomorrow we'll be gone
it's the sound of one hand clappin'
and if ya try and fight it
pilgrim
you're gonna miss the song

CHAPTER 10:

The Ministry Beyond the Ministry

I think of my poems and songs
as hands
and if I don't hold them out to you
I find I won't be touched

if I keep them
in my pocket
I would never get to see you
seeing me
seeing you

and though I know from experience
many of you
for a myriad of reasons
will laugh
and spit
and walk away unmoved
still
to meet those of you
who do reach out
is well worth the risk
    and pain

so
here are my hands
do what you will

Hands by Ric Masten

Having worn the hat of a minister for close to forty years now I'm still not always completely sure when I've got it squarely planted on my head and when I don't. To whatever extent my avuncular advice and counsel to my more freshly minted ministerial colleagues may be, I like to urge upon them that they do not allow their entire identity as a human being to be solely defined as "minister." Find at least a couple of other worlds to move in, I say to them. Find yourself other circles of relationship beyond those of your ministerial life, I tell them.

I've even managed to take my own advice. I do have other worlds in addition to my family and minister life that I can go run around in. They are very important and very meaningful to me. But sooner or later the word gets out in those worlds that I'm also a minister, and the hat shows up. It may not sit as firmly on my head as when I'm in the pulpit, or doing my more definitively "ministerly" things, but it never quite completely falls off either. That's OK. I've long come to accept the idea that even when it's not on my head, my minister hat will still be flopping around on my back, tied to a string around my neck; and at some point it will get noticed. Perhaps the best way to put it is to say that I've managed to create spaces for myself where I can wear my ministerial garb much more lightly than when I'm in full tilt "minister mode."

In Ric Masten's case it's a somewhat different situation. Being a Unitarian Universalist troubadour minister is one piece of the much larger mosaic of his life. It is not the hat he always wears; and there are any number of occasions and circumstances where the hat is scarcely visible at all. But in a larger sense Ric's life is a ministry even when it's not seen or recognized as being overtly such.

The poem *Hands* relates what Ric is saying as a poet to those he tries, and hopes, to reach. A minister could say much of the same thing. Ministry, among many other things, involves extending the hands of those who minister: "...and if I don't hold them out to you I find I won't be touched." Sometimes, as noted in the poem, the extended hand is taken and at other times it is shunned. But Ric's words, "to meet those of you who do reach out is well worth the risk and pain, so here are my hands, do what you will" are ones that any minister can well relate to in living out the many challenges, pains, and rewards of ministry.

In this chapter we will look at some of the ways Ric has extended his hand in settings and situations that go beyond his minister-self. As we've already seen, even before Ric Masten and the Unitarian Universalists discovered each other he was endeavoring to create a career for himself as a speaking poet, folk singer, and troubadour; and was having some success at it. Where his career might have gone had he and the UUs not crossed paths is one of those "what ifs" that will never be fully answered. What did happen, as his Billings Lecture travels gave him heightened visibility from 1968 on, was that he began receiving invitations to speak, sing, and read his poems in a variety of secular settings, particularly in schools of all grades and on college campuses.

The section of his book *Notice Me!* titled "Friends" contains some very moving testimonials from those who witnessed, and were deeply touched, by Ric's appearances in several educational, and other, settings. [Note: I don't know if the people I identify here still hold the positions they did at the time of the writing of *Notice Me!* I cite their positions to put their recollections in context.]

Sherrie Dewey Moritz, a Primary Gifted Coordinator for a Phoenix, Arizona school district, recounts this Ric Masten moment with students in the younger grades:

"I was captivated by the growing warmth of eyes, the opened hearts, the rapt attention and the strong voice coming from behind the podium. I heard stories of personal learning disabilities, examples of terrific and horrible poetry and warnings to tell someone at home they were loved before it was too late. Sure, some struggling teens balked at the harshness of the reminders at them, but softened hearts and introspection were evident."

Ms. Mortiz then describes what she saw as she tagged along with Ric and Billie Barbara to their next immediate stop which was a county nursing home: "I watched the hugs Billie Barbara entered with, the moist eyes of the residents, the toe tapping, and the weakly clapping hands. I sat on the floor with the wheelchairs to join in the event. I could see the value of going from one spoken poem to another, from guitar to voice, from Billie's honesty of personal struggles, to the room briefly coming to life with joy, hope, and faint courage."

Helen Harris, an English teacher in a middle school in Alameda, California tells this story: "What do these kids (junior high age) want with a rumpled nonconformist poet carrying an old-fashioned guitar with no amp? Anyone can see he's not from their planet. But he's done prisons, I remind myself. They must be as bad. But he's not here to entertain, and he doesn't take the easy way out by keeping them laughing. He tells them that his first poem got an F. He tells them about the time he considered suicide, and how writing about it helped. He takes us all the way. In 45 minutes the class has gone from scoffers to celebrants. Past pain to prevailing. He sings, 'I, the caterpillar…so fragile and so frail,' and tears stream down my face, and a few students see and poke others who turn and look. That's okay, though; we are bound together in a shared experience. These pupae of mine—these awkward, scared, overwhelmed kids—have gotten to be, along with me, for a few moments, 'tangled in the strings' of a real poet."

From the other end of the country, David Fowler, the Headmaster of Proctor Academy in Andover, New Hampshire describes an ongoing relationship Ric had with that school for a time. After a few of his appearances on the campus, Mr. Fowler and some of the Proctor students spent ten days at Ric and Billie's Big Sur home in something of a live-in writing workshop: "We did the chores, cooked the meals, took trips up and down that beautiful coast experiencing and sharing and writing." This experience in turn led to Ric being made Proctor's poet-in-residence for a nine-week term. Here's Mr. Fowler's recollection of that time: "We had no plan other than to have Ric weave himself into the educational fabric of the school. Science, history, and English classes shared this poet/teacher's thoughts. He even taught an English elective and read once a week to our school assembly. Ric the poet/magician became the poet/teacher. No more quick, powerful strikes on the minds of the student body and then the quick exit. Now he had to hang around and deal day in and day out with the power of his words and with those wonderfully frustrating, distracting, considerate, irresponsible, and loveable teenagers." The outcome was: "There were minds that were touched. The deepest, most sensitive part of each of us was stirred. It was that window to our soul that was flung open allowing us an opportunity to find new ways to express ourselves. God bless the poet for he allows us to acknowledge the unbroken ribbon of our humanness."

The most pointed of the collection of remembrance essays that are appended to *Notice Me!* is the one titled *Ric Masten: One of Our Failures* by G. Lynn Nelson of Arizona State University in Tempe. He tells of how he introduced Ric as the keynote speaker to the annual meeting of the Arizona English Teacher's Conference in Phoenix as "one of our failures" because "when he (Ric) was in our English classes in junior high and high school we failed Ric with our red pens in our hands and righteousness in our eyes and told him he could not write...we told him he was dumb (and) made him ashamed of his own words; we turned him away from the gift that was in him." Mr. Nelson then went on to explain that it was not dumbness, but dyslexia, that was preventing Ric from putting words on paper in the way they're "supposed" to be written. And then he comes to the point:

THE MINISTRY BEYOND THE MINISTRY

"Ric, then, is one of our failures in another way; we failed him. We failed to help him—because of our own blindness—to see and nurture and develop the gift of language that was in him even then. We did not have to see or believe that he would become a published poet, but we did need to see and believe that the gift of language—as a tool for psychological and spiritual survival—was in him then. Because it was. As it is in all of us, whether or not we can spell."

This was a completely secular setting. At no point was Ric identified as a minister. And yet what took place here was an act of ministry if there ever was one. It was a yet another of those transforming moments that Ric has so often been a party to—in this case before he even spoke a word! A piece of his life was shared in such a way that minds were opened to possibilities that had previously gone unseen. Lynn Nelson summarized the gift of Ric's life and poetry in this way:

"I am glad that Ric is one of our failures. I am glad that he now goes around the country undoing for others what was done to him. I am glad that he gives his gift so freely. He teaches us well. And in our gray stone schools, I hope that we who profess to teach writing are at last beginning to learn the lesson of this poet who is one of our failures."

Not everyone bought Lynn Nelson's message, however. Not all English professors were as convinced of Ric's poetic acumen. Ric knew this himself: "The thing that made me accessible to UUs was what made me inaccessible to a lot of English Departments. They said my work was too thin. I remember at a college in Santa Fe, New Mexico the head of the English Department—he had this long raggedy scarf—and he came up after I'd gotten a standing ovation from the students and said, 'Ric, that was really something. But it wasn't poetry; it was vaudeville.'" Vaudeville or not, Ric goes on to wryly report that when Beacon Press published a collection of his work called *Speaking Poems* it sold 7000 copies.

While there is no concise way to summarize the message Ric has tried to convey to the many students in the many and varied academic settings in which he has met them, these few lines from his poem *This I Would Say to Graduates* come close:

> *for me poetry is trying to put a line of language*
> *around the pain and puzzlement—corralling them*
> *to better comprehend what is troubling me*
> *I don't write about things I understand*
> *I write to better understand about things.*

Ric Masten has moved, and continues to move, in many worlds that both encompass and go well beyond his minister world. His singing poem *Homesick Snail* (which he also named the camper he and Billie traveled in for a time) captures well the spirit of his far flung travels. His note with the song is that it's to be sung for kids in Kindergarten to the 3rd grade, and it clearly works well on that level. But it's also about the home we all seek, and carry somewhere within us, as we move through the many and varied worlds, or gardens, of our existence, wearing the many and varied hats that we do in the course of our travels.

HOMESICK SNAIL

Did you ever hear the story
Of the homesick snail?
You'll find him in the garden
At the end of a tearstained trail.
The ant is in his anthill
The bug beneath the stone
But the snail slips down
That winding road
Tryin' to find his home.

Homesick
Slidin' along

Feelin' homesick
But where
Does a homesick snail belong?

The spider is contented
In her spider web.
The butterfly right at home
Flyin' overhead
And deep within the woodwork
The termite drills a hall
And each and every cricket
Has his hole in the wall

Chorus

The fuzzy caterpillar
Is asleep in his cocoon
The angleworm digs underground
Where there's lots of room
The centipede and beetle
Each have found a place
But the homesick snail
Goes racing round at a snail's pace

Chorus

I guess he's born to wander
Yes I guess that's all he knows
Cause everytime the snail arrives
He thinks it's time to go.
Sliding down that highway
Down his silver track
Searching for the very thing

He carries on his back.

Chorus

*We all live in the garden
And I am the snail.*

Among those wider worlds in which Ric has moved he's come into contact with persons who have, as the expression goes, a "high name recognition factor." Among the various pictures, notes, and poems tacked to the wall of his study is a shot of him and Joan Baez playing together. Ric uses the occasion to poke a little fun at himself.

THE FAN

*you ask
do I know Joan Baez?
Well, let me count the ways*

*it was the summer of '67
in the afterglow
of a Big Sur celebration
she was barefoot
and wore a blue velvet gown
her presence filled the room
and children followed
her around*

*we had a friend in common
who brought us together
laughing as we joggled
cups and saucers
from one hand to the other
her touch was firm and cool*

and though
a hundred years go by
I'll not forget
what Joanie had to say
the day
we held each other
in each other's eye

"Hi"

or are you really asking
does Joan Baez know
that she knows me?

It was on one of his Unitarian Universalist journeys that Ric met up with Pete Seeger. This time it was more than a "Hi"; it was the beginning of an ongoing friendship, and it caused Ric to alter his performing style. They met following a gig they shared at the Fourth Universalist Church in New York City. Ric estimates the time to be a little prior to 1980: "It came my time to sing and I had to bring out my music stand because I couldn't remember my lyrics, whereas Pete and the others could just perform without anything in front of them. I later told myself, 'You haven't cared enough about your folk singing to learn to play the guitar better or to better learn your lyrics. You enjoy the performance part, so why not be a speaking poet and write poems that are supposed to go into your ear and not through your eye.' I wrote him (Seeger) and thanked him for making me a speaking poet, and he wrote back and thanked me.'"

Ric also recounts this from that first meeting:

"After the performance Pete asked me to join him for dinner. His daughter, who had just returned from Mexico was also there, and Pete was excited about seeing her again and wanted to know about her trip. So I sat there and chatted with a fellow from *Folkways Magazine* who had also joined us for dinner. All of a sudden Pete stops and looks at me and says, 'Oh I'm terribly sorry. I'm being very rude, Ric.' It was as if he put a bell jar over the two of us and for about 20 minutes he gave me all of his attention. What I learned from Pete is something I've always tried to be and do myself. He could be the same guy in front of a thousand people as he was just talking to me. Absolutely the same guy—no public persona and private persona. That's what I try to do and be as a speaking poet."

Then there was this interesting part of their conversation: "Pete asked me, 'How in hell did you make it as a folksinger? I came up through the unions.' I told him, 'Well, I came up through the Unitarian Universalist churches.' And he said, 'Ah, liberal religion, of course!" Whether this piece of their conversation had anything to do with it or not, in more recent years Pete Seeger has come to identify himself as a Unitarian Universalist, and has performed at a couple of UU General Assemblies and other UU related events.

The meet-up that Ric remembers most fondly, and that was the beginning of an ongoing friendship, was with Ruby Dee and Ossie Davis. As best he recalls it began over 30 years ago. Ms. Dee was putting together a one person poetry reading show to do on Broadway and her daughter found a copy of Ric's *Speaking Poems* in a New York bookstore. Ms. Dee's secretary contacted Ric for permission to use three of his poems which he was delighted to give. It all led to their having a lunch meeting in Harlem on Ric's next trip to New York City:

"This was when Billie and I were touring together in our *Homesick Snail* camper. It had every religious symbol on it and a poem. By the time we got to the restaurant in Harlem Ruby Dee was already there and all the waiters and waitresses were having her sign menus and napkins. When I came in she asked me to sign my book for her; and all these black people are wondering who this white guy is in this Harlem restaurant, and who Ruby Dee thinks enough of to ask him to sign a book for her! I'll tell you when you hear your poems read

THE MINISTRY BEYOND THE MINISTRY

back to you by someone like Ruby Dee—they were so good I couldn't believe I'd written them!"

This meeting led to yet another meeting on the same trip that ended up giving Ric another of those "what if..." wonderings. Here's how he tells it:

"She (Ruby Dee) said that the man who was producing her show would like to meet me, and could we drop by and visit him after lunch? It was Joseph Papp, but the name meant nothing to me at the time. So we dropped in and he had this elegant place with a grand piano, and was actually wearing a smoking jacket. He looked like Hugh Hefner. He asked me to do my gig—Billie and I—for him and when I finished he asked me what I was doing the following February on such and such a date. He offered to pay my expenses to do two nights at the same club where he had Ruby on. He said that if I were successful he'd like a piece of me, and if not I'd still gotten a free trip to New York out of it. Well, by the time I got back to California I knew who Joe Papp was!"

Then things took this turn:

"By the time I got home I was so freakin' tired, and I looked at February and saw I really couldn't do it then. I asked if I could do it when I'd be back in New York later in that same spring. But Papp didn't want to wait until spring. It was either that February or not at all. So I decided to pass. As it turned out, the day he'd picked turned out to be when one of the biggest snow storms ever hit New York, and shut down the City. So I wouldn't have made it anyway. But I spent many years wondering where that 'no' of mine came from. Was I mostly afraid to go out there and face the New York critics, and find out that I really wasn't much after all?"

It was his long-time friend Ron Cook who, some years later, finally got Ric to put it all in the right perspective: "One day I was walking along with Ron on a Big Sur ridge overlooking the Pacific Ocean, and I told him this story. He asked, 'Suppose you'd gone and it was beyond belief and people loved you and you were the darling of the town and Papp wanted you to leave Big Sur so he could work with you? Would you have moved?' As I thought about it I told Ron I wouldn't have gone. So he told me to quit worrying then because I'd designed a good career for myself and had had it all these years, and all kinds of wonderful things have happened to me."

For all of his far flung travels and contacts, whether wearing his minister hat or not, Ric would probably agree that the most wonderful things that have happened to him have taken place in the area that has been his life-long home. He is a well known presence in the arts and poetry scene in the Monterey Peninsula area where he has offered his readings and concerts in a variety of locales. As noted in the Preface, I was reintroduced to Ric in 2000 by a mutual friend who did not know he was a UU minister, but who was very much aware of his reputation as a local poet and performer. Indeed, his formal—or as formal as it gets—title in the environs of Monterey and Carmel is that of "Troubadour and People's Poet of Carmel."

Beginning in the mid-1990s Ric has become a regular in Monterey's First Night celebrations on New Years Eve. Paulette Lynch, the Executive Director of the Arts Council for Monterey County, and the founder and first director of First Night Monterey, tells of how Ric was recruited into that event: "We met Ric in 1994 through our Board President Fred Hernandez, who was also an editor at the *Monterey County Herald* at the time. At first Ric had no interest. He couldn't imagine people at a big festival coming to see a poet. After a year or two of Fred's gentle but constant insistence, Ric tried us out. He was stunned that not only was the place standing room only, but people stood outside listening and laughing and cheering. He became a wonderful new discovery for many people each year and a perennial favorite for many more."

Still another local honor has come Ric's way from the California State University at Monterey Bay. In September of 2006 he received a letter from the University's President, Dr. Diane Harrison, informing him that he would be presented with an Honorary Doctor of Letters degree at their May, 2007 Commencement. In her letter to Ric Dr.

Harrison wrote, "This Honorary Degree represents the California State University's recognition of your unique contributions through spoken and written poetry. I would also like to extend our campus community's invitation to you to present the keynote address. Your presence would be a distinct honor for our CSUMB community, as well as the residents of our neighboring communities." Not bad for a guy who flunked out of four colleges and dropped out of a fifth!

In a case of one creative soul recognizing the creativity of another, a local photographer, Douglas Steakly, asked Ric to provide some poetry for a hard bound collection of stunningly beautiful photographs of the Big Sur region taken by Mr. Steakly called *Pacific Light* (published in 2000). Big Sur has to be one of the most photogenic places on earth as it is, but Steakley's pictures bring out an even deeper beauty that the eye seldom sees at first glance. The poems Ric wrote to accompany the photographs further enhance their beauty. On a page opposite a picture of a section of Pebble Beach called Bird Rock are these words of Ric's:

> *like the tip*
> *of ebony icebergs*
> *the rocks surface silently*
> *gleaming*
> *the evening sky*
> *streams across*
> *a plane of reflective sand*
> *all that is needed*
> *to complete this picture*
> *is a set of footprints*
> *made my someone*
> *come to bear witness*

And in a photo of Bixby Bridge as seen looking northward from the vantage of Hurricane Point, there is this:

> *looking North*
> *from Hurricane Point*
> *I trace the route Kerouac was on*
> *the highway*
> *Brautigan came down*
> *beginning in the late sixties*
> *a generation of flower children*
> *hitch hiked here*
> *colorful pilgrims*
> *making the trek*
> *to Mecca*

Another poem in the *Pacific Light* collection points to yet another piece of Ric's life where his minister-self and his poet/troubadour-self come together. The picture is that of a waterfall dropping onto a secluded beach. This is the poem:

> *depending on the size*
> *of the wedding party*
> *at exactly this spot on a trail*
> *in Julia Pfeiffer Burns*
> *the nuptial knot is tied*
> *the bridal veil of McWay Creek*
> *seen falling behind and below*
> *the robed officiant*
> *for years now*
> *lovers have come*
> *to exchange their vows*
> *outdoors*
> *here in God's house.*

The "robed officiant" referred to here is Ric Masten himself. Among the various identities he carries in the Monterey/Carmel/Big Sur region is that of officiant, or "Master of Ceremonies," as he calls it, for Big Sur weddings. As described on his website he "strives to create a non-doctrinal affirmation that is spiritual rather than religious." He offers the couple to be joined a site in a wooded area of Big Sur or on the sand of a beach with rocks all around. It's the choice of getting married "in the woods" or "on the rocks" as he puts it. The most intriguing part of Ric's Big Sur weddings is the robe he wears while conducting them. It was made by his daughter, Jerri, from a couple of brown army blankets and is covered with a variety of symbols. The symbols have been created by the couples he's married. In a pre-nuptial meeting Ric gives the couple the robe and asks them to embroider something onto it, or attach something to it, that they feel best symbolizes their union.

Ric has cut way back on officiating weddings now, but during a visit in January of 2006 my wife and I were fortunate enough to attend one. What was supposed to have been an outdoor ceremony was overruled by torrential rain, so the dining room of the Big Sur inn and restaurant where the wedding party and guests were housed had to be used instead. Even in that confined setting it was a wonderful and joyous occasion. His Big Sur weddings are one of the few times when Ric still straps on the guitar Rolfe Gerhart made for him so many years ago; and he had the entire gathering heartily singing along to *Let It Be A Dance* as part of the overall ceremony.

One of the pieces of counsel Ric gives to the couple he's marrying is, "Let us pray that something goes wrong so that you'll have great stories to tell later." I don't know that the rain on that day could be regarded as something that went wrong—it just wasn't part of the plan. But wrong or not I'm sure the couple who were joined on that day will long remember and cherish the memory of their Big Sur wedding where a room full of people sang at the top of their spirits, as the rain pounded on the roof, and as they were led by a rather elderly gentleman with an impish smile and wearing a brown blanket robe with funny looking things all over it. Who could forget that?!

So who, or what, was Ric Masten in that setting? Was he a minister, a master of ceremonies, a poet, a troubadour, a songster...a guy helping a roomful of people have a good time? How about all of the above? The various identities we carry and the hats we wear sometimes have a way of meeting and merging. Ric has a life that goes well beyond his minister life, as we have seen. But when his minister life meets up with some of the other parts of his life it can be a beautiful thing.

CHAPTER ELEVEN:

A Taste of Cilantro

*"Old soldiers never die,
They just fade away."*

Gen. Douglas McArthur

*booking dates
for the one man band that I am
I notice that my hands
are becoming transparent
the names in my Rol-a-dex
showing through ominously
in my ear a voice states
that the number I have dialed
is no longer in service...
that the person
I am attempting to reach
retired last year
or worse
"Oh, you haven't heard..."
it becomes apparent
I will soon need gloves
to find my fingers*

you can't put the flavor
of cilantro into words
or for that matter
phone conversations
it must be tasted first hand
and so even before
the sales pitch was over
I had already disappeared
visible only to the shrinking
circle of my peers
and to the kind of people
who dine in cafeterias

a pity only because
I'm too damn stubborn
to settle for a standing ovation
in Sun City

Old Soldiers by Ric Masten

The above poem was written following a few experiences that have come Ric's way in more recent years. As he tells it, he'll be planning a tour and will put in a call to a church where he'd appeared some years earlier. Instead of getting the minister he'd expected to talk with, however, he'll find there's another one in place now. Plowing ahead, Ric will make his pitch for coming to that minister's church only to be interrupted with the question: "So, tell me again, Mr. Masten, what it is you do?"

"At that point," Ric admits, "I know I'm done…I'm like a taste of cilantro, you can't put into words what I do. You have to taste it."

Ric's very cogent observation captures the irony of this book, in that it is an attempt to put into words what he's been doing as he's traversed the Unitarian Universalist landscape—and gone well beyond it as well—over the past 40 years. We can write *about* what he's done, but we can't put the taste of a Ric Masten moment on paper anymore than words on paper can put the taste of cilantro in your mouth. Cilantro, just for the record, is the leaf of the young coriander plant, and is grown in Ric's native California. It's an herb that can be crushed; and among its many uses is that of a seasoning for Mexican dishes like chili or tacos or enchiladas. Without, I hope, stretching the metaphor too far, Ric has provided some seasoning for our liberal religious movement over the past forty years. He has given it enhanced life and extra spice that would not have otherwise been there.

The taste of anything that crosses our tongue and palate is fleeting. If it is pleasant we can recall with pleasure the experience of tasting, but we cannot relive the taste itself. All that Ric and I have been able to do in these chapters is recount some of the experiences of those who have tasted the cilantro he's offered—and Ric's experiences in offering it. That will have to do when it comes to words on a page. Some who read this have been fortunate and blessed enough to have tasted Ric's magical ministry first hand. For those who have not, we hope that you feel thanksgiving and gratitude for the flavoring he's given liberal religion over the years; and that you, in turn, will find ways of offering your flavorings as well.

Our first chapter opened with the image of a mountain, and we pick up that image again here. If life is a journey, or a hike up a mountain, the critical point on the hike is when we meet ourselves. Ric's ministry has helped any number of people do just that on their journeys of spirit and meaning. Here he has some fun with himself as he muses on his own mountain journey:

ON THE MOUNTAIN

somewhere about a third of the way up
he came striding down the trail
and caught me unaware

a poet
staff in hand—naked—thin as a whip
wild gray hair framing the sun-stained face
his bright eyes blue holes, the sky shining through

when he saw me resting there
he laughed out loud—"Friend," he said
"I have been to the summit and found nothing there!
Absolutely nothing!"
then laughing again he went on down around the bend
and left me

with my brand-new Day-Glo knapsack
ten-dollar compass and waterproof boots
remembering how I'd sharpened my knife
till it shaved the hair off the back of my wrist
preparing myself for almost anything
but this

still I was young then and it wasn't until I too
had run out of places to climb
that I began to wonder where he was going
and what he was after
laughing that way

so turning around
I followed on behind
and if I took you by surprise this morning
coming down the path
believe me, I was only laughing at myself
sitting there

This final chapter is primarily intended to give Ric the last word in our recounting of his remarkable life, both within and beyond the UU ministry. True to form he has offered his concluding words to this work with a series of poems, including the one that opens this chapter. Closing in on one's 80th year, even in the absence of a cancer diagnosis, tends to make personal mortality something other than an abstraction. What hasn't changed for Ric, however, is his penchant for finding playful ways of dealing with weighty matters, as the following poem demonstrates:

ME AND PANCHO VILLA

approaching 80
with a life threatening disease
the conversation with my peers
often steers itself in the direction of death
not morbidly but with a natural curiosity

of course
everyone works it out in their own way
"Whatever gets you through the night,"
I always say
"Just as long as you don't come after me with it!"
true believers are off to roll around heaven all day
the reincarnation bunch have round trip tickets to punch
which might also be OK as long as I don't have
to remember this one

to me the eternity of time that preceded my conception
is of no concern
so why fret about
a return to that non-threatening state
the anxiety
I do have around death has more to do

with being forced to leave the movie
while it is still playing

considering my demise
brings to mind a photograph
of the bandit Pancho Villa
sombrero pushed back—posing for the camera
cartridge belts crossing his chest
here and there a round missing
how did he spend them
were they put to good use
on a hunt—in a fight
or fired aimlessly into the air

the concern here is in my bandoleer
the finite number of shells I have left to fire
before I retire into that long, long dark
I fear that I might spend these precious days
Missing the mark

Then, in a more pensive vein he offers this:

CONTEMPLATING ANKH

when the thrust of my creativity
has only to do with self esteem
when the trophies I have collected
are for me and not the team
when my every action
is intended only to impress
when the collected reams of reviews
are the kind that applaud and rave
all the of above will go with me to my grave

was based on something I didn't choose

I arrived predetermined
gifts and talents, DNA, IQ, disposition
all of which begat the artist
that begat the actor/playwright
that begat the troubadour
that begat the poet
that begat the minister
adding up to the master of ceremonies
I am now

I ask myself how lucky can you be?
able to make a good livelihood
by assisting the creation
of unforgettable moments
for audience and congregation
but most of all
for the couples I have danced with
on the beaches and rocky promontories
that grace the Big Sur coast
Ethan and Kathryn
"I now pronounce you husband and wife"
and by saying so help shape the future
for someone who doesn't believe
that my choices are free
I rejoice in the life that has chosen me

ISBN 1425126081